The Repair and Reupholstering of Old Furniture

BARNES LARGE TYPE EDITIONS

The Repair
and Reupholstering of
Old Furniture

Vernon M. Albers

South Brunswick and New York:
A. S. Barnes and Company
London: Thomas Yoseloff Ltd

Library of Congress Catalogue Card Number: 69–13029

A.S. Barnes and Co., Inc.
Cranbury, New Jersey 08512

Thomas Yoseloff Ltd
108 New Bond Street
London W1Y OQX, England

First Printing of Large Type Edition 1974
Second Printing of Large Type Edition 1976

ISBN 0-498-01597-1 (Large Type Edition)

Printed in the United States of America

Contents

Introduction

There are several reasons for an interest in the repair and refinishing of old furniture.

The reason may be sentimental. You may have inherited a family heirloom which you would like to preserve but unless it can be made a useful addition to your home there is no point in preserving it. Your guests can never feel at ease if they know some of your heirloom chairs are likely to collapse if they sit on them.

The reason may be economic. It is often possible to purchase a nice piece of old furniture, in dilapidated condition. The piece can then be repaired and refinished to become beautiful and useful after a considerable expenditure of effort, but a relatively small expenditure of money. The work involved can be a pleasurable experience and may eventually lead to an interesting hobby. The pleasure derived from such experience will increase as you develop your skills. Each project will be a new and different challenge to your ingenuity. It is important that you take the time to carefully analyze the job to be done, and then do it well so that you can take pride in your accomplishment.

Perhaps the most important reason for an interest in old furniture is that it is particularly attractive in the modern home. The more elaborate lines of the old furniture provide a more desirable atmosphere in a modern house than the simple rectangular lines of modern furniture such as "Danish Modern." We live in a modern house and nearly all of our furniture is either old furniture which has been repaired and refinished, or reproductions of old pieces which I have constructed.

One does not need a large selection of tools to repair furniture, but there are certain tools which are essential for some of the operations, and others are just nice to have. As I discuss the various kinds of operations in repair work, I will suggest the necessary and desirable tools to use. I do not recommend that you go out and purchase a large selection of tools, but rather that you purchase individual tools and materials as you need them. I have a fine collection of tools which I have accumulated over a period of nearly forty years. However, most of my tools were purchased when they were first needed. I strongly recommend that when you purchase a tool you select one of good quality and then take care of it. Have a place to keep it so that you can find it the next time you need to use it. You will not save money by buying cheap tools, and their performance will usually be unsatisfactory.

You will need a place to work. The requirements will depend on the kind of repair you expect to do. Glue, paint remover, or finishing materials will ruin rugs or other floor coverings. It is impossible to prevent some dripping, and it is difficult to control newspapers on a floor so that all critical areas are covered all of the time. Upholstering and chair seating can, however, be done anywhere you can find the necessary space. A basement or garage is a satisfactory place to work for all operations which cannot be done safely in the house.

If you purchase old furniture to repair, you should examine it carefully to determine if the necessary repairs can be made, and if you will be willing to live with the piece after it is repaired. Remember, there is both good and bad old furniture. It is poor economy to waste time and materials on a piece which was worthless when it was originally manufactured. The choice will have to depend on your judgment and good taste.

It is not necessary for a piece to be made of fine wood to be good, if it is the kind of piece which should be painted. There are many fine pieces of pine furniture in which the use of such woods as walnut or mahogany would have been inappropriate. You should consider whether the piece, when it is repaired and refinished, will be attractive and will be a desirable addition to your home.

1

Dismantling

Let us assume that you have a piece of furniture that you wish to repair. Examine it carefully. Are there loose joints which need to be reglued? Can the original finish be retained? Is it upholstered?

Removing the Upholstering
It is unusual to find an upholstered piece that does not need recovering. Since it is impossible to do any but the most minor repairs with the upholstering in place, the normal first step with an upholstered piece is to remove the old upholstering. This should be done very carefully to avoid damaging the wood outside the area covered by the upholstering material. It is important in this process that you pull out *all* tacks. Most workers use a small screwdriver for this operation, but I have found that a small "diagonal cutter," used by electronic technicians for cutting wires, is a very effective tool for this purpose and it is much safer to use than a screwdriver. It is particularly effective for removing tacks that have the heads broken off. *Never use a chisel for this job*. First, it will

ruin the chisel, and second, you are almost certain to injure yourself.

You should always have available a small piece of soft wood, such as white pine, to place under the screwdriver or the diagonal cutter in order to prize out the tacks without bearing the metal tools against the finished part of the wood.

The general principles of upholstering will be treated in Chapter 5, but you will find that each piece of upholstered furniture is, to some extent, a special problem. You should carefully note how the original craftsman did the job. If the piece is complicated, it may be desirable to make some notes with rough sketches to refer to when you come to that stage in the rebuilding. It is also important for you to save the original upholstering pieces to use as patterns when you cut your new material. You should also save all padding. Sometimes portions of the old padding can be reused and the old padding can serve as a model for the preparation of new padding.

Separating Loose Joints

The piece should now be carefully examined to determine if there are any loose joints. Even though a joint may appear to be only slightly loose, it should be separated and reglued. Remember that if a joint is free to move, ever so slightly, additional strain will be imposed on all of the other joints during normal use. This is particularly true of a chair.

Figure 1.1 schematically shows a typical joint. Figure 1.1 A shows the joint reinforced with dowel pins, while Fig. 1.1 B shows a mortise and tenon joint. If the joint is reinforced with dowel pins, part *a* will have its end cut to conform with the surface of part *b*. There will be matching holes in the two parts and hard maple pins, which fit snugly into the holes, that were glued in place at the time the joint was made. The mortise and tenon

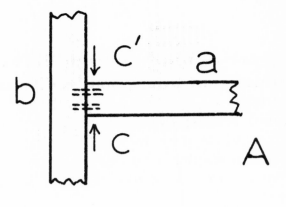

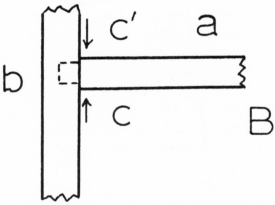

Fig. 1.1 Schematic drawings of typical furniture joints: A, a dowel pin reinforced joint and B, a mortise and tenon joint.

joint shown in Fig. 1.1 B has the tenon cut as an extension on part *a* which fits snugly into a rectangular hole in part *b*.

It is not possible to determine which kind of joint was used until the joint is partially separated. In either case, it is usually necessary to separate the joint an inch or more before the pins or tenon are out of their holes. It is obvious that it will sometimes be necessary to break apart a sound joint in order to disengage a loose joint.

Before attempting to separate the joint, examine it very carefully to be certain that no nails have been driven into it in an effort to reinforce the joint. The removal of such nails is very difficult, and is best accomplished with the diagonal cutter. If the nail was driven in through a finished surface, it is impossible to remove it without some damage to the surface. Your problem is to get it out with a minimum of damage, but you *must* get it out. You are likely to break or damage a vital part if the nail is not removed before you try to separate the joint.

You can sometimes pull a joint apart with a little wiggling in the process, but often more drastic measures are necessary. The most effective persuasion is to tap sharply at points c and c' in Fig. 1.1. This should be done with a wooden mallet and a piece of soft wood held on the surface to be tapped to prevent injury to the wood.

When all loose joints have been separated, carefully clean all old glue from the surfaces including the dowel pins or tenons and the holes into which they fit. If dowel pins were used to reinforce the joint, the pins will usually remain in one part or the other. Check to determine if they are still solidly glued in place, and if so do not disturb them. However, if they can be wiggled remove them so that they can be reglued.

Sometimes dowel pins are broken and have to be replaced. To remove the ends of broken pins from the holes, drill an undersized hole down the center of the pin and with a small chisel gradually enlarge the hole until all of the dowel pin is removed. Do not try to drill out the full diameter of the dowel pin, as you cannot center your bit accurately enough, and the resulting hole will not match with the one in the other part of the joint. Broken dowel pins are easily replaced by cutting the proper length from a piece of dowel pin stock of the proper size which you can purchase at a hardware store or lumber yard.

Occasionally one encounters a joint that is so difficult to pull apart that reasonable tapping with a mallet is not sufficient to separate it. Rather than pound so hard that the wood will be bruised, even with a protective soft wood block, it is better to force the joint apart by driving in a wedge of hard wood. The wedge should be started in a region away from the finished surfaces and should generally be driven in the directions indicated by the arrows in Fig. 1.1.

Removal of Old Finish

When you have separated all of the loose joints and cleaned off all old glue, it is time to decide whether it will be necessary to refinish the wood. If it is possible to retain the old finish, by all means do so. If the old varnish is still clear so that the color and grain of the wood shows through, but it is somewhat scratched and marred, it often can be rejuvenated by rubbing down with linseed oil and a little powdered pumice stone. A piece of furniture will be more attractive for showing the normal signs of wear than it would be clothed with a new, shiny, unmarked finish.

A piece may appear to need refinishing because of an accumulation of dirt and wax on the surface. Before deciding that the old finish must be removed, try washing with soap and warm water, and then rub a portion of the surface with a piece of cloth which has been dipped in turpentine. If you can preserve the old finish, you will not only make the job of repair much easier but you will have a more attractive piece of furniture. You can do much to rejuvenate an old finish, after the old wax is removed, by rubbing it with linseed oil. However, if the varnish has become opaque or the piece has paint on it which you wish to remove, it is often easier to do the paint or varnish removal while the piece is dismantled.

I prefer to remove the old finish with one of the commercial paint and varnish removers. You should strictly follow the directions on the container, paying particular attention to the procedure for removal of the last traces of the chemical at the end of the process. Remember that if some of the paint-removing chemical remains on the surface of the wood, your new finish will never harden when you apply it later.

The commercial paint and varnish removers do not disturb the grain of the wood appreciably. Do not sand the surface of the wood at this time as it is desirable that you remove as little as possible of the original surface of the old wood.

Tools Required for Dismantling

The tools required for dismantling a piece of old furniture are a wood mallet, a small screwdriver, a diagonal cutter, and a small piece of soft wood about ⅛ inch thick. If you break a dowel pin, you will need a small drill or wood bit (about ¼ inch) and a ¼ inch or smaller chisel to dig the remainder of the dowel pin out of the holes after you have drilled a hole down the center. A good pocket knife is satisfactory for scraping off the old glue.

2

Assembly

After you have separated all loose joints and carefully scraped off all of the old glue, you are ready to reassemble the piece by regluing all joints that have been separated. This is a very important operation. A properly glued joint makes the two parts effectively one piece. No relative motion of the two parts is permitted as long as the glue holds. A properly glued joint is stronger than the adjacent wood.

The strength in a glued joint is a function of the accuracy in the fit of the parts. This is particularly true of the animal glues used on old furniture, but even the modern plastic glues will form a stronger joint if the fit is tight than if it is loose and sloppy. This is one reason for the importance of adequate clamping to insure that the mating surfaces make intimate contact with a film of glue between them.

Preparation for Assembly

It is essential to have everything ready when you start the process of gluing, as the joint must be clamped within

17

a few minutes of the time of application of the first glue. The only way to determine if everything is ready is to go through a dry run, including clamping the joints to be certain that they go together properly. I can think of nothing so sad as the predicament of the eager beaver who starts to glue a piece only to find that he has replaced a dowel pin with one that is too long, or has had a scrap of something get into a dowel pin hole or a mortise so that the joint will not quite go together.

Gluing

We must now consider the order of assembly. It is seldom practical to assemble an entire piece in one operation, especially if all of the joints have been separated. Most furniture pieces have four legs with one or two connecting elements between each pair of legs. Figure 2.1 is a simplified example. After making a dry run with legs 1 and 2 with the two connecting elements a and b, this part can be glued. It will be necessary to use two clamps, one to pull the legs 1 and 2 together along the line of the axes of elements a and b. You must have a good square available to ascertain that legs 1 and 2 make right angles with elements a and b. However, if the unit was designed so that the legs are not parallel to each other, the corners will not be 90° so they cannot be checked with the square. If such is the case, you can cut a piece of cardboard with the proper angle during the dry run. It can then be used for checking when the unit is glued.

This is a good place to say something about clamps. It is absolutely necessary to have adequate clamps if a successful glue job is to be achieved. It is possible to purchase clamps which can be made up to various lengths with standard ¾ inch gas pipe. A minimum of four clamps are needed and pipe lengths of two feet, four feet and six feet can be obtained from any plumber. The pipes should be threaded on both ends with standard pipe threads. Do

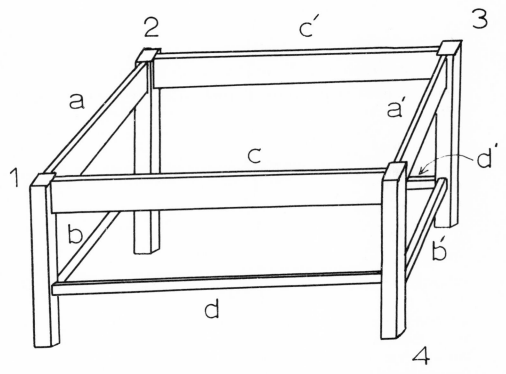

Fig. 2.1 Simplified diagrams of a typical piece of furniture.

not attempt to use a clamp that is so long that the weight of the projecting end will pull your work out of shape.

All clamps have metal shoes which engage the wood. These clamp shoes will produce ugly scars on the wood surfaces unless wood blocks are placed between the shoes and the wood. It requires three or four hands to apply the clamp and hold the wood blocks in place. I have solved this problem by drilling two holes in each clamp shoe with a No. 25 drill and attaching wood blocks to the shoes with No. 6 wood screws. Of course, the screws must be short enough so that they do not extend all the way through the wood blocks.

Let us now assume that you have made a successful dry run with legs 1 and 2 of Fig. 2.1 with the elements *a* and *b*. After removing the clamps and placing them where they can be easily retrieved, you are ready to apply the glue. I prefer to use white plastic glue which comes in plastic squeeze bottles. Apply the glue to all surfaces as rapidly as possible, then put the joints together. After this apply the clamps and check with your square or your special cardboard to verify that the unit has been drawn together properly. The four legs of the finished piece will not all touch the floor if you glue the unit together crooked. Be certain that the clamp bars are parallel to the elements *a* and *b* and that the clamping forces are directed along the axes of *a* and *b*. If you apply a clamp between *a* and *b* the legs will be curved due to the force of the clamp, and they will remain curved when the clamp is removed. When you apply the glue, avoid an excess but always apply the glue to both of the mating surfaces. Later, I will describe a method of dealing with curved legs.

When the section is properly clamped, wash off any glue which has squeezed out of the joint with a rag and warm water. Although the glue will set in about half an hour, you should not do any work with the newly glued section until the next day because it takes several hours for the glue to attain its full strength.

After the section involving the legs 1 and 2 is glued, follow the same procedure with the section consisting of legs 3 and 4 and elements *a'* and *b'*. When these two sections are finished and the glue has been allowed to set for at least 24 hours, they can be joined with the elements *c, d, c'* and *d'*. Four clamps will be required for this final step, and there are eight joints to which glue must be applied before clamping. Don't forget to check all four corners for the proper angles. Also choose a level place and check to be certain that all four legs rest on the floor.

Clamping Sections with Curved Legs

We have considered the simplest example, one in which the legs are straight. We often encounter pieces with curved legs, as shown in Fig. 2.2. If you try to apply a clamp shoe at *A*, keeping the clamp bar parallel to the element joining the two legs, it will slip down. This can be prevented by clamping a block *B* to the leg with a

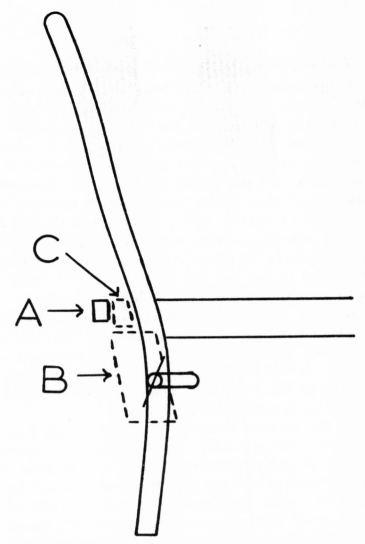

Fig. 2.2 Method of clamping sections of furniture with curved legs.

C clamp. Once again be sure to place a small wood block on the other side of the leg to prevent the C clamp from marring the wood. A second small block *C*, cut to approximately match the curvature and angle of the leg, will help to distribute the clamping force and prevent damage to the surface of the wood.

It is impossible to anticipate every possible shape of furniture to be assembled. But if you will follow the general principles which have been described and use your ingenuity, you can work out a method of clamping any kind of structure by experimenting with dry runs so that you will know exactly what you are going to do after you have applied the glue. Be certain that your clamps will not pull the structure out of shape when they are tightened to draw the joints together. It may be necessary in some instances to cut temporary wood braces to hold an element so that the clamps will not pull it out of shape. This can be determined during your dry runs. Any such bracing must be prepared before the glue is applied.

Repairing Breaks

We have considered above the procedure for assembling a structure which is undamaged. Frequently we encounter pieces which are damaged and repairs are necessary in addition to regluing joints. It is not possible to anticipate every kind of repair, but I will describe some that I have made. With these descriptions you should be able to work out methods of repair for any damage which you may encounter.

The first example is a common form of break where the top of a chair back is attached to the top ends of the back legs by a glued joint reinforced with a dowel pin. If the glue on such a joint fails and a heavy person leans too hard on the back of the chair, the wood may break out along the dotted line labeled "break" in Fig. 2.3. The break follows the line indicated because that is the direction of the grain of the wood. In order to repair a break of this kind, I glued the broken piece back in place on top of the leg. There was then a dowel pin hole about an inch deep which served as a guide for a wood bit used to bore the hole about two inches deeper. A longer dowel pin was then used when the joint was reglued. That repair was made about ten years ago and has shown no sign of failure although the chair has been in constant service.

It is not uncommon for a chair or table leg to be broken

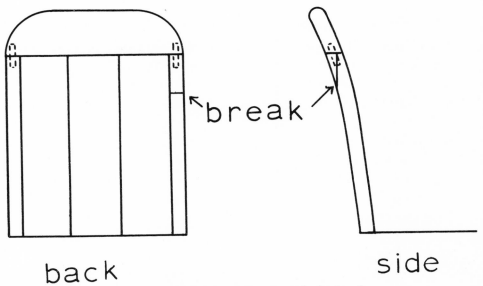

back   side

Fig. 2.3 Typical break in a chair back.

at a point where it has been turned down to a small diameter. This can be repaired by boring a hole along the axis in both directions from the break. The area of the hole should be at least one-half the area of the leg at that point. The holes should be made deep enough so that a dowel pin can extend at least two inches into each piece. The pieces are then assembled with the dowel pin glued into the holes.

If the grain of the wood runs diagonally to the length of the leg and the break occurs along the grain of the wood, the parts can be glued together without the use of a dowel pin. The area of the wood in contact is great enough so that no reinforcement is necessary.

Figure 2.4 A shows a broken chair leg that was a particularly difficult repair job. At first, one might be tempted to create a new leg to replace the broken one, but the difference between new and old wood would always be obvious.

Examination of this break indicated that the original craftsman who fabricated the chair made the mistake of boring the hole for the round element about 3/4 inch too

Fig. 2.4 A. Photograph showing the two parts of a broken chair leg before repair.

B. Photograph of the chair leg glued together before reinforcement is added.

C. Photograph of the chair leg with reinforcing block and rectangular hole cut to receive the reinforcing block.

D. Photograph of the chair leg with the reinforcing block glued in place.

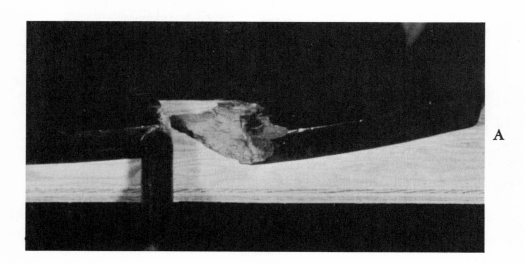

A

B

C

D

deep causing the leg to be weakened at that point. In order to repair this leg, I decided to glue it and then add reinforcing. Figure 2.4 B shows the leg after gluing but before the reinforcing was added. To accomplish this second step, I cut a rectangular hole about 2¾ inches long and as wide as the cavity beyond the end of the round.

Figure 2.4 C shows the leg after the rectangular hole was cut and the wood block for reinforcing which fits into it. The block was cut from a piece which matched the wood of the chair as nearly as possible. Figure 2.4 D shows the leg after the wood block was glued in place and smoothed down until the surface was ready for refinishing.

This is an example of the addition of reinforcing after preliminary gluing. It would have been very difficult to drill a dowel pin hole in the two pieces accurately enough to be effective. Although this repair will always show to some extent, it is not serious and can be compensated for by the fact that the leg is probably stronger than before it was broken.

Another instance where it is advantageous to add reinforcing after gluing is in making or repairing picture frames. The moulding of which the frame is made is cut at an angle of 45° and the corner is accurately glued in a right angled jig. Figure 2.5 shows the arrangement for gluing. After the glue has set, a hole is drilled at A so that a dowel pin can be glued in to reinforce the joint. By following this procedure it is quite easy to glue the sections of the moulding together accurately. The glue holds

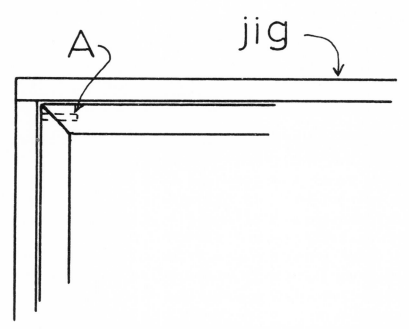

Fig. 2.5 Method of gluing the corner of a picture frame and adding a reinforcing dowel pin.

them solidly in place while the hole for the reinforcing pin is drilled.

Table Tops

You are fortunate if the top of a table you are rebuilding is not warped. Often table tops are warped so that the top is convex and the bottom is concave, although this may be reversed.

The reason for the warping is unequal distribution of moisture in the wood. The side which has the higher moisture content will be convex because of the greater swelling produced by the moisture.

Before attempting to correct the warping, you should remove the old finish. It is difficult to change the moisture balance to correct the warping because if you try to do it too rapidly the wood may crack.

In order to correct the warped condition it is necessary to remove moisture from the convex side and, possibly, add some to the concave side. A good place to treat the table top is on a cement floor in a basement or garage. Such a cement floor is poured on the soil and is, therefore, slightly damp. Place the table top on the cement floor, concave side down, and suspend a string of 100 watt electric lamps above the top over its most convex portion. Adjust the position of the lamps so that the wood surface is noticeably warm. The time necessary to correct the warping varies greatly with the kind of wood and its age. Pine will respond very rapidly while a hard wood like cherry will react more slowly. The progress should be watched closely to be certain that the warp does not reverse itself. It is desirable to turn off the heat overnight to allow the moisture time to redistribute in the top surface since you will not be able to heat it uniformly. During hot weather you can lay the top on the grass, convex side up, and let the sun warm the top surface. Be sure to take it inside at night. When the top is flat, stand it on end and check each day to be certain that it does not start to warp again. If it does, repeat the process. It may take a while to completely stabilize it.

Occasionally the glued joints in a top will be separated. Most old tops have the pieces glued together with dowel pins for reinforcing. If the glue has failed so that the joint can be separated, pull it apart and then carefully clean off the old glue. Using clamps to draw the joint together, join with white plastic glue. If there is more than one joint in a top to be reglued, they should all be done at the same time. If there is warping to be corrected, this should be done before the joints are reglued. It is usually necessary to hold the top flat when the joints are drawn together with the clamps by placing wood strips along each side of the top, perpendicular to the glue joints, and clamping these with C clamps. This should be done at each end of the top and the C clamps should not be fixed securely until the main clamps have been finally tightened. To prevent fixing the strips to the top with glue which squeezes out of the joints, wash off the excess with a rag and warm water, and place waxed paper or plastic food wrap between the strips and the table top.

Special Reinforcing

It is sometimes desirable to add some special reinforcing to an old piece of furniture, if it can be done without the reinforcing showing when the piece is finished. Upholstered chairs, sofas, and tables are the kinds of furniture which may need supplementary reinforcing and which can be strengthened without the reinforcing being evident when the rebuilding is completed.

One method of adding reinforcing is shown in Fig. 2.6. The block A is carefully cut so that its surfaces make good intimate contact with the sides. The screws B hold the block in place. After the screw holes have been made and you verify that they will draw the block firmly into con-

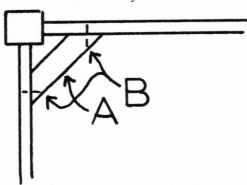

Fig. 2.6 Corner reinforcement in a piece of furniture.

tact with the sides, remove the screws and coat with glue the ends of the block and the areas where they contact the sides. Put the block back in place drawing the screws up tightly. The glue is most important, as a block held only by screws adds very little to the strength of a corner joint.

3

Finishing

Preparing the Surface for Finishing

If you did not have to dismantle the piece, you will now need to decide if the old finish can be retained. This was discussed in Chapter 1 and you should refer to that section if you are considering removal of an old finish.

Any deep gouges or nail holes should be filled. If these are small, they can be filled with paste wood filler to which a small amount of the appropriate pigment has been added. (*See* the discussion about wood filler and pigments in the next section.) The paste wood filler should not be diluted with oil when it is used to fill holes. The necessary pigment should be worked into it with a small wooden paddle until it is uniformly distributed. On occasion, I have eliminated the oil and turpentine from diluted filler which was left after filling the wood surface. This was done by allowing it to settle over night and then carefully removing some of the residue from the bottom of the container and placing it on a folded paper towel. The paper towel will soak up the excess oil and turpentine, leaving the residue on the surface. The residue can then be used to fill the holes. They should be filled so that the material is more than ample as it will shrink when it dries. Paste wood filler should be used only for small holes, and they can be filled after the filler has been applied to the wood surface.

Larger holes can be filled with a mixture of glue and sawdust, or better still a mixture of glue and sandpaper dust. Do not use the white plastic glue for this. The best glue to use is the powdered variety which you prepare by mixing with water. Mix the glue according to the directions on the container, then add a little more water so that the mixture is quite fluid. Add sawdust or sandpaper dust while stirring until the mixture is stiff and then fill the holes with a knife blade or a small screwdriver. Heap the filler in the hole to allow for shrinkage and when it is hard, sand it flush with the adjoining surface. Large gouges are best filled with wood. Cut out the damaged area to a depth of $\frac{1}{16}$ inch or more, depending on the depth of the damage, and cut a piece of wood to fit the damaged area. The wood should match the old wood as nearly as possible and should be just slightly thicker than the depth of the hole. Glue in place and sand down flush with the surface. The grain in the repair piece must run in the same direction as that of the adjoining surface. *See* Fig. 2.4 D for an example of such a repair.

Before applying any kind of finish, except paint, be certain that all glue is eliminated from the wood surface. This is important because the finishes penetrate the wood while glue will prevent the penetration. The surface appearance where glue has been left will show much greater contrast with the rest of the surface after finishing than before.

Plastic wood is very easy to use for filling holes as it can be purchased in collapsible tubes ready to use. The walnut plastic wood works quite well with walnut, and the colorless plastic wood is satisfactory to use with maple. However, with other woods such as cherry and mahogany the color match is usually not acceptable, though it is a very convenient filler to use if the piece is to be painted. The plastic wood shrinks considerably as it dries, so it should be heaped up and then sanded down flush after it dries. This may take a day or two if the hole is deep. Filling with a glue and sawdust mix or plastic wood must be done before applying any finish. If holes are to be filled with paste wood filler, it can be done after applying filler to the surface but before the final finish is applied.

Varnish Finish

Varnish is the most commonly used finish on old furniture, and it is the most desirable finish to use if you have a dust-free room for finishing. Any dust which falls on the varnish before it dries will stay on the surface.

There are many good furniture varnishes available and most varnish manufacturers supply the varnish in both glossy and flat finish. The varnish finish on old furniture is almost never glossy because it was either rubbed down to a flat finish at the time of application, or the gloss has been removed by many years of polishing. Because of this, an old piece with a glossy varnish finish simply does not look right. It is too obviously refinished.

If you decide to refinish with varnish, and you have removed the old finish with a paint and varnish remover, you should be certain that all of the residual paint and varnish remover has been eliminated. Follow the directions for the particular brand you have used. You may be tempted to sand the piece vigorously to remove all of the blemishes in the wood. You should carefully consider if this is desirable. If the blemishes, due to normal use, are not too unsightly, it may be better to allow them to remain in order to preserve the old surface of the wood. You will need to sand the surface very lightly with a very fine sandpaper or a medium grade of steel wool to eliminate the slight raising of the grain by the paint and varnish remover. If it is necessary to sand down the surface to remove unsightly blemishes, use a medium grade sandpaper and finish off with fine sandpaper.

If the surface of the wood is porous, it may be desirable to use a filler to build up the pores before varnishing. The filler should be prepared by using paste wood filler which is similar to putty with oil to keep it soft. A portion of the filler should be removed from the container and placed in a dish with some linseed oil and a small amount of turpentine. Work up the mixture with a small wooden paddle until the suspension of filler in oil and turpentine has about the consistency of thin cream. You should start with a small amount of oil and turpentine and when the filler has been worked into the liquid, gradually add linseed oil until the desired consistency is attained. Some pigment should be added to produce a color as near as possible to that of the wood as it will be when oil is applied to it. Pigments in oil can be obtained from your local paint dealer in small collapsible tubes and should be added in very small amounts. It takes very little pigment to produce the amount of color needed. Burnt umber will produce the proper color for walnut; burnt umber plus burnt sienna will be about right for most mahogany. You can obtain several of the reds and browns so that by the proper combination, any color of wood can be matched.

The filler should be applied to the wood with a cheap varnish brush. Do not use your good hog bristle varnish brush to apply the filler because it is difficult to clear the solid particles of filler out of a fine bristle brush. When the surface becomes dull due to absorption of the oil by the wood, rub it with old rags until the only remaining filler is that which is in the pores of the wood. If the piece of furniture is large, do not try to do all of it at one time. A great deal of hard labor is required to rub the filler down to the wood and it must be done before the oil has had time to dry. About 24 to 48 hours after the last filler was rubbed down with rags, rub the entire surface with fine steel wool to be certain that all filler on the surface of the wood is removed. After rubbing with steel wool, carefully wipe the entire surface, especially all corners, with a clean rag to be certain that all particles of steel wool are removed. Any particles embedded in your varnish are very unsightly.

A note of caution is in order here. The filler contains linseed oil, and the rags which you use to rub it down with will become saturated with the oil. The linseed oil oxidizes in the presence of air, generating heat and if the oil coated rags are wadded up, the heat will be retained. It is easily possible for them to get hot enough to ignite. You should *always* spread out linseed oil coated rags for a few days to be sure that they do not spontaneously cause a fire.

It is not necessary to use wood filler prior to varnishing, and if the wood is white, such as maple, it is better not to use it as the oil in the filler will darken in time. With white woods, it is better to fill the pores of the wood with varnish. This is done by applying successive coats of glossy finish varnish and sanding down each coat with fine sandpaper until the only remaining varnish is that which is retained in the pores of the wood. If a flat finish varnish is to be used, it will be used only for the final coat. The varnish should be brushed, parallel to the grain, until it ceases to flow down to form ridges of extra thickness.

I have never been able to find a sufficiently dust free area to get a dust free varnish finish so I generally use glossy finish varnish and then rub down the final coat with linseed oil and powdered pumice stone. The powdered pumice stone is added to a small amount of linseed oil in a saucer and a cloth pad is dipped into the mixture and used to rub the varnished surface until a smooth flat finish is obtained. The tiny dust particles which settled in the varnish will be ground down so that they will not show.

The surface should be examined quite frequently to be certain that you do not cut all the way through the varnish to the wood. At least two coats of varnish should be applied before rubbing down with oil and pumice stone. Each coat, except the last, should be lightly sanded with fine sandpaper. Of course, it is important that the varnish be thoroughly dry before it is rubbed down or sanded. When you have rubbed the surface to the desired texture, wipe the oil and pumice stone off with a clean rag, wash your hands and get another clean rag and carefully wipe the surface again. If you do not follow this precaution you are apt to have some permanent finger prints on the finished surface. Also remember the precaution about spreading your linseed oil coated rags out to dry before putting them in the trash can.

You should never dip your brush directly into the varnish can as this carries air into the varnish. This air will cause a scum of oxidized varnish to form and the next time you use varnish from the container, it will have particles of scum in it which will ruin the finish. You should pour some of the varnish from the container into a dish, such as a saucer, and any which remains in the dish when the job is finished, should be discarded.

Do not try to save money by buying a cheap varnish brush. The only satisfactory brush for use with varnish is one made from genuine hog bristles. A brush about two inches wide is best suited for furniture varnishing.

Since a good varnish brush costs between $2.00 and $4.00, it is important that you take proper care of it. The brush must always be thoroughly cleaned *immediately* after use. If you decide to leave it until the next day for cleaning, you might just as well throw it into the trash can as it will be worthless for any future use. It is actually quite easy to properly clean a varnish brush or any paint brush. I use a small dish, similar to a cereal dish, for a two inch brush and give the brush six or seven rinsings, each in two or three ounces of clean turpentine. The turpentine is poured into the dish and the brush is worked in the turpentine until it has had a chance to work over the entire length of the bristles. The turpentine is then discarded. After the series of rinsings with turpentine, wash the brush in warm water with plenty of powdered soap or detergent. It will take considerable soap or detergent to neutralize the turpentine, so be sure to add enough so that good suds will remain after the final washing. Finish by rinsing the soap out of the brush with clear warm water and hanging it up to dry. The above procedure may sound complicated, but if you have everything organized it will take between five and ten minutes to clean a brush. Brushes cleaned in this way will improve with use. I have two hog bristle varnish brushes which are several years old and they are softer now than when they were first purchased. If the brush does not have a hole in the handle, drill a small hole so that you can hang it from a nail. This will prevent the bristles from becoming deformed in storage during periods when the brush is not in use.

Shellac Finish

Although shellac is not as durable as varnish for a wood finish, it is often used on furniture which is not exposed to rough usage. White shellac can be purchased at any paint store. The commercial shellac is dissolved in methyl alcohol but the solution is too concentrated for use as it comes from the container. It should be diluted 1:1 with shellac thinner which is methyl alcohol.

Finishing with shellac is similar to finishing with varnish and any filling of the wood is done in the same manner as for varnish. The action of the shellac, however, is different from that of varnish. Varnish dries by oxidation of the oils in which the resin is dissolved, while shellac dries by evaporation of the alcohol leaving the shellac as a deposit in and on the wood. If it is used in concentrated solution it will not have an opportunity to penetrate the pores of the wood before it dries and will, therefore, remain on the surface so that it can be easily chipped off.

About three coats of shellac should be applied using a good hog bristle varnish brush. The surface should be lightly sanded between coats, and the final coat should be rubbed down with the finest grade of steel wool unless a glossy finish is desired.

The shellac dries much faster than varnish so it is necessary to work rapidly in order to get a smooth job. The procedure for cleaning the brush is similar to that for cleaning a brush used with varnish, except that shellac thinner is used instead of turpentine. Because the dried shellac can be redissolved in the shellac thinner, the brush can be recovered if the shellac is allowed to dry on it. However, redissolving the dried shellac is a slow process so it is much easier to clean the brush if it is done immediately after use. When you do the final washing with water, it is not necessary to use soap because the methyl alcohol is soluble in water; however, it is important to rinse the brush a sufficient number of times with the shellac thinner to remove all the shellac because it will not remain in solution in the alcohol water mixture. Do not discard the shellac thinner used to wash the brush. Save it in a separate container to use later for thinning shellac.

Although white shellac is usually used for furniture finishing, there are some instances where the brown color of orange shellac is desired. It is sometimes used on maple when it is desired to simulate the color of old maple which has been finished with an oil finish. The same procedure is followed in using orange shellac as that described above for white shellac.

You should always work in a well-ventilated area when using shellac and you should avoid getting the shellac on your hands. The methyl alcohol used as a solvent for shellac is a poison and inhaling too much of the vapor is dangerous. The natural oil on the skin is soluble in methyl alcohol so it is possible for it to be absorbed into the blood stream through the skin with extended contact.

Lacquer Finish

Lacquer behaves much like shellac when it is applied with a brush except that it dries even faster than shellac. It should be lightly sanded between coats and the final coat should be rubbed down lightly with the finest grade of steel wool if a flat finish is desired. A lacquer finish scratches more easily than a shellac finish so it is not very desirable for furniture which will be subjected to rough usage.

It is difficult to get a good glossy finish with lacquer applied with a brush because it dries so fast. If a glossy finish is desired, it is better to spray the lacquer on the surface. It is now possible to purchase clear lacquer in aerosol pressurized containers which can be used to spray the lacquer directly on the surface to be finished. Be sure that there is nothing around which will be damaged by the lacquer and be careful to provide adequate ventilation. Of course, if a glossy finish is desired, the final coat should not be rubbed down with steel wool.

Use lacquer thinner for cleaning the brush and save the used thinner for use in thinning lacquer. Normally you should use the lacquer as purchased but the solvent evaporates quite rapidly when the container is open so it is sometimes necessary to thin it. Finish cleaning the brush by washing with soap and water.

The lacquer thinner evaporates rapidly and the vapor is very inflammable so always work where there is good ventilation and avoid any open flame in the area where you are working.

Paint Finish

There have been many instances where pieces of furniture constructed of fine woods such as walnut, mahogany or cherry have been found under a number of coats of paint. Such furniture was not originally intended to be painted but the paint was applied by people wishing to cover an old varnish finish which had deteriorated because they did not know how to refinish the piece with varnish, or the piece was to be used in a place where painted furniture was more appropriate. This has apparently been responsible for the notion, held by many, that an old piece of furniture must always be finished so that the natural color and grain of the wood shows. As a result of this misapprehension, there are many old pieces which were originally intended to be painted and which would look much better painted, that are now finished with various transparent finishes so that the "natural" grain of the wood shows. This is particularly unfortunate when we consider that the enamels now available, in either flat finish or glossy finish, are superior to those available to the early craftsmen and we also have a greater selection of colors than they did.

If the piece has paint on it, it will nearly always be necessary to remove the old paint because you will usually find that the old paint is chipped and a chipped place will always show regardless of the number of coats of new enamel that are applied.

The preparation of the surface for painting is similar to that for varnishing except that it is not necessary to add any pigment to the filler and holes can be filled with any convenient material such as plastic wood. After the filler in holes and blemishes has solidified, it should be sanded down flush with the wood.

The first coat of paint should be enamel undercoat. When this has dried, you will find that the grain of the wood has been raised slightly so you should rub it down smoothly again with steel wool to provide a smooth surface for the enamel.

The enamel is essentially the same as varnish, except for the fact that it contains pigment, so the procedure for applying it is the same as that for applying varnish. A good hog bristle brush should be used and the enamel should be brushed sufficiently so that it will not run on the surface. Two coats of the enamel are usually required to adequately cover the surface and the first coat must be thoroughly dry before the second coat is applied. The procedure for properly cleaning the brush is the same as that for cleaning a brush which has been used with varnish.

Oil Finish

A linseed oil finish is desirable for use on any of the dark woods such as walnut, cherry or mahogany. Filler may be applied in the same manner as for varnish finish. After the oil in the filler has dried for at least 24 hours after the filler is rubbed down with rags, rub the surface lightly with fine steel wool and carefully wipe off all particles of the steel wool.

Prepare a mixture of about ⅓ turpentine and ⅔ linseed oil and apply the mixture liberally to the surface with a brush. Any cheap paintbrush is satisfactory for this purpose. You will notice that the oil pentrates into the wood more rapidly in some places than it does in others but allow two or three hours for it to soak in and then rub down with rags. Finish by washing your hands and doing a final polish with a clean rag. After a coat of oil has been rubbed down and polished it should be allowed to stand for at least 24 hours before the next coat is applied. At least three coats will be required before you will note that very little of the oil is soaking into the wood. You should then finish with one or two coats of a mixture of equal parts of linseed oil, varnish and turpentine. These coats should be rubbed down in the same manner as the others but when the mixture containing varnish is used you should start rubbing about an hour after application to be sure that the varnish does not start to dry before you finish rubbing it.

Remember this precaution, though: spread the oil-soaked rags out to dry so that they will not start a fire. The best rags to use are cotton such as pieces torn from old sheets or cotton shirts. Rags of synthetic fibers such as nylon or rayon are practically worthless for rubbing an oil finish.

If you are finishing a large piece, it may be advisable to apply the oil to only a part of it at one time as the physical labor involved in properly rubbing it down may be too great for you if you try to do it all in one operation.

When fine gunstocks are finished with oil, a filler is usually not used and a sufficient number of coats of oil is applied to completely fill the pores of the wood with the dried linseed oil.

French Polish Finish

French polish is a finish that is a combination of shellac and linseed oil. It is applied with a pad of cotton wrapped in a piece of cotton cloth about six inches square. The cotton pad is soaked with shellac and the cotton cloth is wrapped around it so that the excess of cloth forms a handle. The ball formed by the cotton wrapped in the cloth is then dipped lightly in linseed oil and the wood surface is rubbed with it. As the rubbing progresses, shellac squeezes out through the cotton cloth, which is wet with linseed oil, and the shellac is rubbed into the pores of the wood where it dries by evaporation of the shellac solvent. When the ball begins to stick to the wood it should be dipped in the oil again and, as the shellac in the cotton becomes depleted, more shellac should be added. When you stop work, polish the surface with a clean rag to remove any excess oil.

With this finish, the shellac is being used as a filler and the polishing should be continued until the pores of the wood are filled. A good job of French polish on a large piece of furniture requires a great deal of work but it produces a very fine finish.

4

Chair Seating

Introduction

Chair seats may be cane, split reed, or rush, in addition to upholstered. We will cover the procedures for upholstering chair seats in the next chapter. The kind of chair seating to be used is determined by the construction of the chair. For example, a chair designed to be caned must be caned, as it is impossible to apply any other kind of seat to such a chair. In some instances, either rush or split reed may be used on a chair but the style of the chair will usually indicate which is more appropriate. If the front and back horizontal members on which the seat is formed are not at the same level as the side horizontal members, rush seating cannot be used. However, if all four of these members are at the same level and the front legs project at least one-fourth inch above the tops of the horizontal members, rush seating can be successfully used. A chair which is designed to be upholstered must be upholstered again and one which was not designed to be upholstered should not be upholstered.

Since all of the forms of chair seating are relatively easy to do, and the materials are quite inexpensive and easy to obtain, there is no good reason to spoil a chair by using the wrong kind of seating material.

Many people seem to think that there is some sort of magic in the art of chair seating and that it is difficult to learn. Actually it is one of the arts which can be taught to the mentally retarded. The quality of the job which is done depends more on the care which is exercised than on any special skills.

Old chairs often have a fiber or wood solid seat nailed in place over an old cane, rush or split reed seat that has worn out. This kind of repair is obvious when you examine the bottom of the seat.

Cane Seating

Cane for chair seating comes in three widths—fine fine, fine, and medium. The width of cane to be used is determined by the size of the holes and the spacing between holes in the chair seat. A chair designed for the fine fine cane has holes about $\frac{3}{16}$ inch in diameter spaced about $\frac{3}{8}$ to $\frac{7}{16}$ inch between centers. If the holes are spaced approximately $\frac{9}{16}$ inch between centers, use the fine cane and if the spacing is approximately $\frac{3}{4}$ inch between centers the medium cane should be used. Do not try to use a wider cane than the hole spacing indicates, as there will simply not be enough space to weave the cane into the pattern.

Cane can be purchased from companies that supply educational materials to industrial arts departments in schools. One such company is the J. L. Hammett Company Kendall Square, Cambridge, Massachusetts. These companies can supply either natural cane or plastic cane. I have used both and I find the natural cane much more desirable than the plastic cane. It produces a much more attractive finished job and it is just as easy to work with as the plastic cane.

The natural cane comes in packages of about 1000 feet and the length of the individual canes is from about six to twelve feet. I usually sort out five or six lengths of the cane, roll them into coils, and place the coils in a pan of cold water. The water softens the cane so that it is less likely to break or crack when it is bent around sharp corners.

There are seven separate steps in caning a chair seat. Figure 4.1 shows the first step completed. The chair illustrated happens to have front and back rails with the same number of holes, so that one end of the cane was inserted in the right-hand hole of the back rail until the end projected through the rail about three inches. The cane was oriented so that when it was pulled forward, the glossy side was up and a wooden peg was inserted into the hole to hold the cane in place. The other end of the cane was then passed through the right-hand hole in the front rail and it was pulled through so that there was no slack in the cane but it was not stretched tight. (You should be

Fig. 4.1 Illustration of the first step in caning a chair seat.

careful not to have any twists or kinks in the cane. The cane has a high tensile strength but can be broken easily if you pull on it when it is kinked.) Another wooden peg was inserted in the hole through which the cane was passed in the front rail to hold the cane, and the free end was passed up through the second hole in the front rail and drawn tight keeping the glossy side up. The wooden peg was then moved over to the second hole and the process repeated back and forth until the remaining end of the cane was not long enough to reach across the front-to-back span of the chair seat. A second length of cane was then started in the next hole with a wooden peg to hold it and the process was continued until the condition illustrated in Fig. 4.1 was reached.

The chair which I have used for the illustrations happens to have the same number of holes in the front and back rails. However, it is more usual to find that the back rail has a smaller number of holes than the front rail. Suppose that you find that there are 17 holes in the back rail and 19 holes in the front rail. You should start the cane in the right-hand hole in the back rail and bring it forward to the second hole from the right-hand side in the front rail and then continue as I did in the example illustrated in Fig. 4.1. When that is completed, a short piece of cane can be added between each of the end holes in the front rail and a hole in the side rail selected so that this piece of cane is parallel to the rest of the cane in the seat.

The ends of the cane which are being held by the wooden pegs can now be anchored by pulling them under the loops that pass from hole to hole on the underside of the rails.

Figure 4.2 shows the seat of the chair with the second step of the caning completed. This was done in a manner similar to that of the first step except that the cane was threaded from side to side instead of from front to back.

Figure 4.3 shows the seat with the third step completed.

Fig. 4.2 Illustration of the first and second steps in caning a
chair seat.

Fig. 4.3 Illustration of the first, second and third steps in caning a chair seat.

In this case the cane was threaded in the same manner as in step one. We now have three layers of cane. The bottom layer runs from front to back, the middle layer runs from right to left and the top layer runs from front to back. These first three steps are very easy but the work from now on becomes more difficult as in the next step we will start the process of weaving the pattern.

The fourth step consists of threading cane from side to side parallel to the cane of the second step. However, at each pair of the front-to-back strands of cane the cane is passed over the one in the top layer and under the one in the bottom layer. The cane installed in this step should be woven on the same side of the canes of step two in all of the rows. In most instances it does not make any difference which side is chosen so long as they are all the same. Figure 4.4 shows the seat with step four completed. In this case the

Fig. 4.4 Illustration of the first four steps in caning a chair seat.

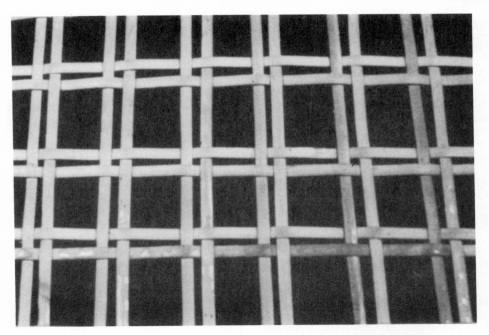

Fig. 4.5 Enlarged detail of the pattern of the first four steps in chair caning.

space between the first side-to-side row at the front and the front edge of the seat is greater than the space between the last row at the back and the back edge of the seat so the canes installed in this step were put on the front side of the canes of step two. Figure 4.5 shows a detail of the pattern at the junctions where step four was completed.

Figure 4.6 shows the seat with the first cane of step five

Fig. 4.6 Illustration of the first four steps in caning a chair seat with the first cane of step five in place.

in place. In step five the cane is woven diagonally. I started this cane at the right-hand front corner and at each corner of the pattern formed by the cane of the first four steps the cane was passed under the pair in the side-to-side rows and over the pair in the front-to-back rows. Figure 4.7 shows the seat with step five completed and the first cane of step six in place. Figure 4.8 shows an enlarged detail of a portion of the pattern.

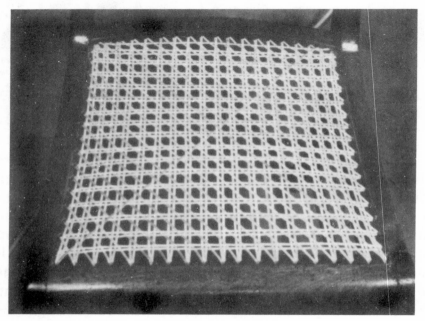

Fig. 4.7 Illustration of the first five steps in caning a chair seat completed with the first cane of step six in place.

Step six is woven in the same manner as step five except that it is woven on the diagonal perpendicular to that for step five and the cane is woven over the side-to-side pairs and under the front-to-back pairs.

The trim which covers the holes around the seat is applied as in step seven. Two pieces of cane are used. One piece lays along the edge over the holes and the other is

Fig. 4.8 Enlarged detail of the pattern of Fig. 4.7.

passed up through each hole, over the top cane and back down through the same hole. It is then passed underneath to the next hole and the process is repeated until the top cane is locked down at all of the holes around the seat. Figure 4.9 is a photograph of the completed seat. You will usually find that the holes are becoming rather full by the time you get to step seven and you will need something like a slender punch which can be pushed through the holes to push the canes aside to make room for the cane of step seven.

When step seven is completed all loose ends of cane under the rails should be tucked under loops and the excess cut off. If any of these ends appear to be slipping out of place, they can be permanently anchored with a drop of white glue.

A job such as this may appear complicated as you read this, but if you cane a chair, following the above instructions step by step, you will be surprised at how easy it is. This is a clean job which can be done while you watch

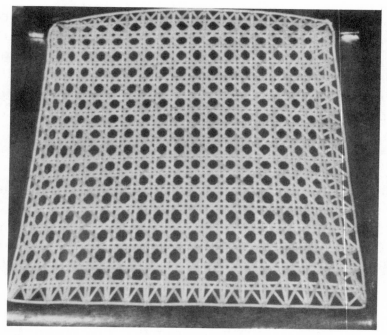

Fig. 4.9 Illustration of a caned chair seat with all seven steps completed.

television. A chair, such as the one used in this example, can be done in six hours or less. If you do not tell your friends how simple it is they will be impressed with your skill.

Some chairs have shapes that are more complicated than the one used as the illustration. In some cases it may be desirable to locate the center holes in the back and front rails and start with these for step one and then work from there to each side remembering that all canes in step one must pass through properly selected holes so that they are parallel with each other and spaced about the same distance apart. Follow the same procedure with step two. You will find that there is no particular difficulty even if the seat is circular.

Some old chairs have cane backs as well as cane seats. There is no fundamental difference between caning a chair back and a seat. However, many of these chairs are constructed so that the cane shows on the back where it passes from hole to hole. It is therefore necessary to use much more care to keep this neat than it is on the underside of the seat which does not show. You should, therefore, anchor all cane ends in the holes with glue and then clip them off close.

Split Reed Seating

Split reed comes in widths of $\frac{3}{16}$, $\frac{1}{4}$, $\frac{3}{8}$ and $\frac{1}{2}$ inch. The width of split reed to use for a given chair depends on the design and size of the chair. A large rugged chair will be more appropriately seated with the $\frac{1}{2}$ inch reed while a small, old fashioned kitchen rocker will look best with the $\frac{3}{16}$ inch reed. The width of reed to use on a given chair is a matter of judgment. A difference of $\frac{1}{16}$ inch is certainly not critical. The split reed can be purchased from the same sources as cane seating.

Before starting to weave the seat, you should sit down with pencil and paper and work out the design which you wish to weave in the seat. The weaving with split reed is very simple. Start one end of a reed at the back rail next to one leg of the chair. The end of the reed can be attached to the inside of the rail with a tack with some white glue between the reed and the rail. (The finish should be scraped off at this point so that the glue will stick to the wood.) After the end of the reed is secured pass it over the top, around the front rail, underneath the seat, and over the top again. This wrapping around is continued until you reach the other end of the split reed. If you reach the end as the reed is on top of the seat, cut off enough so that the next length of reed can be spliced to it underneath the seat. A convenient means of splicing the reeds is to overlap them about an inch, apply some white glue, and tie them together with a piece of string or wire to hold them together until the glue dries. The narrower split reed is glossy on one side. If there is a glossy side, wind the reed so that the glossy side is out. Do not wind the strands of reed so close together that there will not be sufficient space to weave in the right-to-left reeds. The space required will depend on the pattern you have designed and the coarseness of the reed you are using. It is better to leave more space than is necessary between reeds than to wind them so close together that they will buckle when the right-to-left reeds are woven in to form the pattern. The front-to-back reeds should not be wound tight as they will become tighter as the pattern is woven.

When the seat is covered with reed wound from front to back, it is time to start weaving the pattern with reed wound from left to right. The end of the first reed is woven into the front-to-back reeds for a few inches on the underside of the seat. There will be sufficient friction to hold the end in this way. The other end of the reed is woven across the seat of the chair according to the pattern which you have designed. The ends of all reeds can be secured on the underside by weaving them into the front-to-back reeds.

You should do any necessary refinishing of the chair before installing the seat, as the rails must be finished the same as the rest of the chair because they will not be completely covered by the reed. It is not necessary to weave the complete pattern on the underside of the seat but it is desirable to do some weaving on the underside to hold the layers together.

Figure 4.10 is a photograph of a split reed seat which I did with $\frac{3}{16}$ inch reed. This seat has been in service for about 35 years. Figure 4.11 is a photograph of the seat of a large chair in which $\frac{1}{2}$ inch split reed was used. I did this seat about ten years ago. It is obvious that split reed seats last for many years, they are very easy to do and the material is quite inexpensive. There is, therefore, no good excuse for spoiling a nice old split reed chair seat by nailing a solid seat over it.

Fig. 4.10 Photograph of a split reed chair seat which was done with 3/16 inch split reed. This seat has been in service for about 35 years and should be redone as some of the reeds are broken. The chair will be re-painted before a new seat is woven.

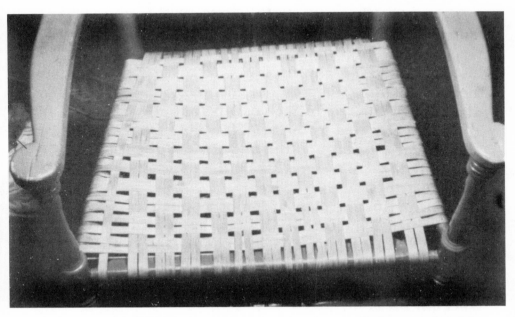

Fig. 4.11 Photograph of the seat of a large chair seated with 1/2 inch split reed.

Rush Seating

Chairs designed for rush seating must be made with the front and back rails on the same level as the side rails. Although split reed seating may be applied to chairs with the front and back rails at the same level as the side rails, most chairs which were designed for split reed seating have the front and back rails slightly lower than the side rails.

Rush seating may be natural or artificial. The natural rush material is formed from the long fibrous leaves of the plant known as cattail millet which grows in swampy areas in the temperate zone. The leaves are dried or the dry leaves may be purchased from sources which supply materials such as cane and split reed. The long narrow leaves are twisted in a rope of $\frac{3}{16}$ to $\frac{1}{4}$ inch diameter and the rope is made continuous by adding leaves to maintain a uniform diameter. The artificial rush is made of a specially treated paper which may be purchased in coils with the paper already twisted to form a rope.

Considerable skill and patience are required to form a uniform rope of natural rush, so an amateur will produce a better appearing seat if he uses the artificial rush. I have used the natural rush only on one chair and I found considerable difficulty in maintaining a uniform diameter of the rope. However, I believe that if one would do two or three chairs he would develop the necessary skill to produce a nice appearing seat.

Both the natural and the artificial rush produce seats which last for years and the process of winding the seats is quite simple.

Most chair seats are narrower in the back than in the front. The first step in winding such a seat is to carefully measure the lengths of the back and front rails. If the difference in these lengths is *a*, lay off a distance equal to $\frac{1}{2}$ *a* measured from the leg toward the center on each end of the front rail and mark these points. The distance between these marks will then be equal to the length of the back rail.

Attach a piece of rush rope to the inside of the left-hand rail, near the front, with a tack and a drop of white glue. Bring the rope forward under the front rail, up in front of the rail, down inside the left front leg and under the left side rail. Now bring it around and over the rail, across the seat parallel to the front rail and under the right side rail, thence around this rail, inside the right front leg and under the front rail. It is then brought around over the rail and attached near the front inside of the right side rail. The rope should be pulled tight before fastening.

Figure 4.12 is a photograph showing this step completed. The photographs illustrating this process were made using a small model which was constructed for the purpose of illustration. A white cord was used to simulate the rush

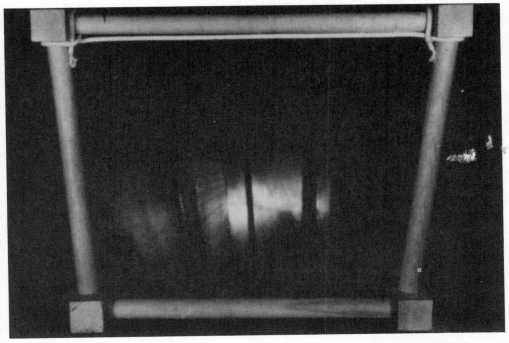

Fig. 4.12 Photograph of a model of a chair seat illustrating the first step in forming a rush seat.

rope and the model was scaled so that its linear dimensions were related to those of an existing chair approximately as the diameter of the cord used was related to the diameter of a rush rope. A series of pieces of rope are installed in the same manner as the one shown in Fig. 4.12 until the front rail is covered from the legs out to the marks, leaving an open space on the front rail equal to the length of the back rail. Figure 4.13 shows the model with this step completed.

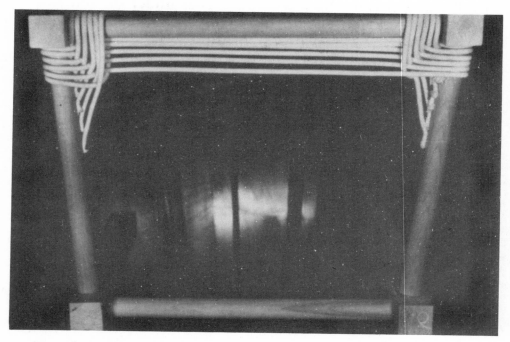

Fig. 4.13 Photograph of a model of a rush chair seat with all of the short lengths of rush in place.

When the above step is completed, the end of a piece of rush rope is attached to the inside of the left rail in the same manner as the preceding short pieces were attached. If natural rush is being used, this rope will be relatively short, not over two or three feet, because you will be forming the rope by twisting in new leaves as you progress but if artificial rush is being used, the piece should be at least 25 feet long. The rope is passed under the front rail, around the rail and over it, inside and under the left side rail, around and over it, across the front and under the right side rail. It is then wrapped around and over the rail, down inside and under the front rail, around and over the front rail, across from front to back and under the back rail next to the right back leg. It is then brought around and over the back rail and inside the right back leg and under the right side rail, around and over the right side rail and across the back where it passes under the left side rail next to the left back leg. It is then brought around and over the rail and passed inside under the back rail, around and over the back rail and passed from back to front parallel to the left side rail and under the front rail. You have now made one complete circuit around the chair. Continue this process around and around to build up the pattern. Most chairs have side rails which are shorter than the back rail so when you have completed the winding to the point where the side rails are completely covered there will still be an uncovered section in the center portion of the back and front rails. This part is completed by winding from front to back. The rope goes under the rail around and over and then under the opposite rail. This is continued until the seat is completely covered.

Along the diagonal lines extending toward the center from each corner where the rope crosses over from top to bottom of the pattern there are more thicknesses of rope per unit length than there are along the rails. It is important to wind the rope tight and push the turns tight together along the rails. This requires that the rope must be squeezed where it crosses so that it will be thinner at the point of crossing than it is where it passes around the rails. The rope is pliable enough so that this can be accomplished but it is necessary to push it together each time it crosses over in order to keep the pattern smooth.

As the pattern is built up the space between the top and bottom layers should be stuffed with soft paper so that the load on the seat will be distributed between the top and bottom layers. Figure 4.14 shows the model with four turns around the seat. The cord used in this model is a very hard cotton cord so it could not be compressed at the points on the diagonals where it crosses over from top to bottom so the pattern is not smooth along these diagonals as it will be when the rush rope is used.

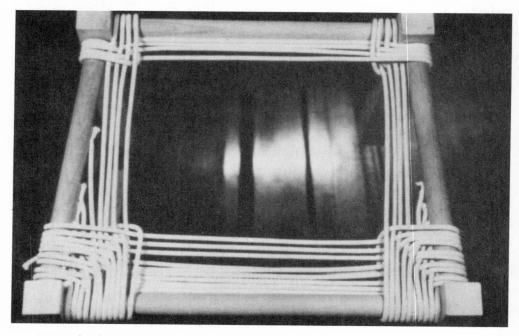

Fig. 4.14 Photograph of a model of a rush chair seat after completing four complete turns around the seat.

The above description may seem complicated but the process is actually quite simple. Before starting your first rush seat, I would suggest that you practice a few rounds with a piece of string so that you can get the procedure fixed in your mind.

If you use natural rush, it is possible to do the entire

seat, after the preliminary short pieces necessary to cover the excess length on the front rail, with a continuous length of rope. When artificial rush is used, it is not practical to start with a long enough piece to do the entire seat, so lengths of 25 or 30 feet should be used. The lengths can be spliced on the underside of the seat by overlapping the

Fig. 4.15 Photograph of a rush chair seat which has been in service for several years.

ends an inch or so and wrapping with string after applying some white glue. Figure 4.15 is a photograph of a chair seat of artificial rush which has been in service for several years.

5

Upholstering

Introduction

In this chapter, we will consider all furniture with which upholstering fabrics are used. The simplest example is the small chair with a padded seat covered with fabric; the more complicated example is the large chair or sofa with a built-up seat containing springs and padding covered with fabric. The large upholstered furniture containing springs in the seat may also have springs in the back but the arms will be padded without springs and in some instances there will be only padding in the back. There is also an intermediate type of chair with fabric covered padded seat with a padded back covered with fabric but with a considerable part of the frame of the chair exposed.

In a book such as this, it is not possible to show how to solve every upholstering problem. This is the reason for my suggestion in Chapter 1 that you should note how the original upholstering was done. Careful observation and note-taking during dismantling can be of great help when you come to the job of building up the padding and, particularly, when you approach the job of fitting the fabric over the padding. You may reach the point on a job where you feel that it is impossible to get a smooth tight fit of the fabric. Always remember that the former craftsman did it and you can do it but it may take much time and patience. As a beginner you should never try to do an upholstering job on a schedule. If you try to do a quick job of fitting the fabric you may get a bad fit or, worse, you may ruin a valuable piece of fabric by cutting too deep at some point.

If you buy a new overstuffed chair or couch of good design with good upholstering, you may pay several hundred dollars for it. A major portion of the cost is in the upholstering fabric and the craftsmanship necessary to properly apply it. As an amateur, you can do as well as the professional but it will take you longer to do it. You have one important advantage if you dismantle the chair yourself. You can see how the professional craftsman solved each of the problems and you can use his pieces of fabric as patterns with which to cut your material.

As I indicated in Chapter 1, you must remove all tacks used in the original upholstering. Old tacks left in the wood can cause more difficulty than that of removing them. Because of the effort necessary to upholster a piece of furniture, you should plan on a job which will last a long time. You should, therefore, be certain that all necessary repairs to the wood frame are carefully done and you should use good materials. You will probably find that the description of the procedures for upholstering large pieces of furniture is quite complicated. If you have never upholstered such a piece, you should not attempt to learn the entire process from the descriptions, but rather, you should go through the process, step by step, reading the description for each step as you do it. It is quite important for a beginner to do his first job on a piece which he has an opportunity to dismantle himself. Every piece is different, in some respects, from every other piece, and the knowledge which you can obtain during the process of dismantling is, therefore, very important. I learned upholstering entirely from the process of taking the old pieces apart. Since I had no instructions to help in the process of rebuilding, I made mistakes, but this is an effective, if hard, way to learn. The information which you can acquire by carefully dismantling your pieces, combined with the following instructions, should prevent you from making any serious mistakes.

There is a great temptation to rip the old upholstering off as quickly as possible and throw it in the trash can in order to get on with the job. This is the wrong procedure for a beginner. You should not only take the upholstering and padding off piece by piece making notes with sketches as you proceed, but you should carefully preserve every piece of fabric and every section of padding. Often portions of the old padding can be used again, but even if they cannot you can use the old sections of padding as models for forming the new ones.

Upholstering Small Chair Seats

Small chair seats are relatively easy to upholster. There are no springs and the padding is supported on jute webbing. The first step in the process is to stretch and tack the webbing in place on the frame of the seat.

There is no substitute for regular furniture webbing, as an especially strong material is required to support the load on the seat and it is necessary to stretch the webbing very tight. It is impossible to impart adequate tension to the webbing without a webbing stretcher. Figure 5.1 is a sketch of a webbing stretcher which can be purchased. There are places where you can purchase upholstering kits which include a webbing stretcher, curved and straight upholstering needles, a magnetic tack hammer, and a tack puller. You may wish to make your own webbing stretcher but it is so inexpensive to purchase that I feel that this is a

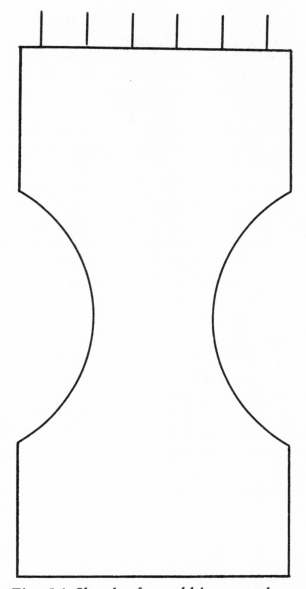

Fig. 5.1 Sketch of a webbing stretcher.

false economy. Sears Roebuck and Company lists the complete kits and they also list some of the components as separate items.

Figure 5.2 is a schematic of the arrangement of the webbing on a typical chair seat. The first end of the webbing is placed over the frame so that its end extends about an inch beyond the point where it should be tacked. It is tacked to the frame with four No. 12 or No. 14 tacks

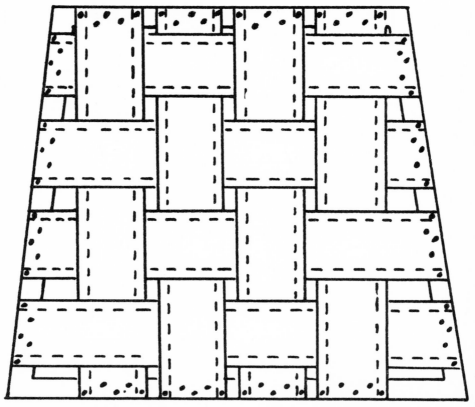

Fig. 5.2 Sketch of a small chair seat with webbing in place.

depending on whether the wood is hard or soft. The short end is then folded over the tacks and four or five more tacks are driven through the two thicknesses of the webbing. The webbing is then stretched with the webbing stretcher as shown in Figure 5.3. While holding the webbing stretcher down, tack the webbing to the second rail with four tacks. The webbing stretcher is then disengaged and the webbing is cut off about an inch beyond the tacks and the end is folded over the tacks and four or five more tacks are driven through the two thicknesses. Note—do not cut the webbing before stretching. Figure 5.4 is a photograph showing the process of stretching and tacking webbing on a larger piece of furniture.

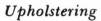

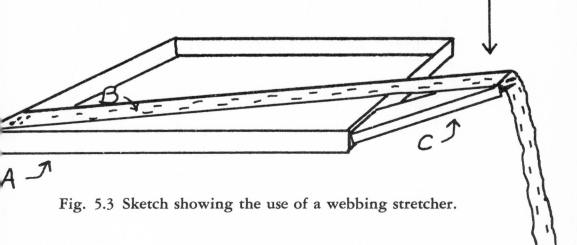

Fig. 5.3 Sketch showing the use of a webbing stretcher.

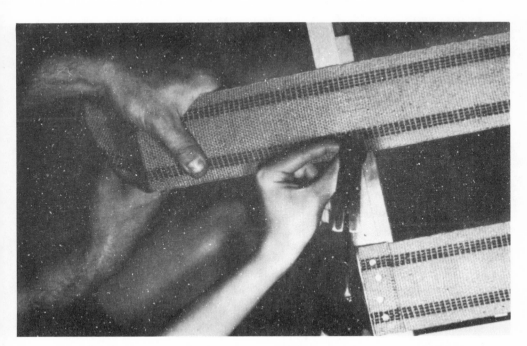

Fig. 5.4 Photograph showing the use of a webbing stretcher.

When the webbing is tacked in place, a piece of burlap should be cut and tacked in place over the webbing. The burlap serves to prevent the padding material from working through between the webbing strips. The burlap should be tacked in place with No. 3 or No. 4 tacks with a space of about 1½ inches between tacks.

The padding may be moss, rubberized hair, or plastic foam. If moss is used, care should be exercised in making certain that there are no lumps. The plastic foam is a relatively new material which is inexpensive and very easy to use. It is available from Sears Roebuck and Company under the trade name of Serofoam in thicknesses from ½ inch to four inches. If plastic foam is used, the one inch thickness will be suitable for most small chairs and the foam can be easily cut to fit the seat. The rubberized curly hair is attached to a base and the pads come in one inch thickness. This material is also easily cut to fit the chair seat. Any of the three kinds of padding is satisfactory and the choice may depend largely on which material is most readily available.

When the padding is in place it should be covered with upholstering cotton which is ¾ inch to one inch thick. The cotton should be cut to about the same size as the pad and the edges should be smoothed down with your hands so that they taper from the full thickness to a thin edge with the edge extending over the edge of the padding. The pad and cotton are then covered with unbleached muslin. The muslin should be stretched over the padding in the same way that you will stretch the final fabric. You should use the same care in stretching the muslin over the padding as you will use in stretching the fabric. There are two reasons for this. The first is that you want the muslin covering to be as smooth as possible because any awkward folds are apt to show through the upholstering fabric and the second is that stretching the muslin over the padding and tacking it in place will serve as a dry run for the fitting of the final fabric. The following procedures, therefore, apply to both the muslin and the upholstering fabric.

Use the original fabric piece for a pattern to cut the muslin and the fabric but allow about one inch all around the pattern. Do not cut the notches for the back legs until you start to fit the fabric around them.

Place the fabric symmetrically on the pad and be certain that the fabric pattern runs in the desired direction on the chair seat. Stretch the fabric from back to front along the center line and fasten with a tack in front and back. Do not drive these tacks down tight as you may need to pull them out and relocate them later. Stretch and tack along lines about three inches on each side of the line of the first two tacks. Keep the fabric tight and if there is pattern in the fabric be careful to keep it symmetrical on the seat. Now repeat the process across the seat from left to right.

You are now ready to fit the fabric around the back legs. At each back corner, cut the fabric with a scissors in a direction toward the opposite front corner. You should cut a little and then try pulling the fabric into place. The fabric must go down between the pad and the inside corner of the leg. If the cut is not deep enough it will not be possible to pull the fabric down tight over the pad but if you cut too deep, the cut will show. When the cut is deep enough, fold the cut edge under on each side of the leg so that it will be tight along the edge and the fold is right at the leg. Drive a tack as close to the leg as possible. When you have the fabric fitted properly around the back legs and secured with tacks, check the fabric at the other tacks to determine if the tension in the fabric is uniform. If it is uniform, drive the tacks down tight. The fabric should be tight enough to compress the padding so that it will not become slack after a few months of use.

You are now ready to fold the fabric around the front corners. Pull the fabric snugly along the side and around the front corner far enough so that the edge of the fold, where the fabric passes from the top over the front edge, will be exactly at the corner. This is easier to do if you pull the fabric from the side around the front and drive a tack through it into the front edge. The fold is then tacked as near to the corner as possible. Remember that the fold must be made and secured so that the fabric is tight over the padding and also tight along the side and front edges.

When these folds are secured, work around the chair adding tacks until there is a tack about every two inches in the muslin but the tacks securing the fabric must be close enough together so that the pattern of the fabric does not appear to have waves between tacks. The size of the tacks to be used will depend on the wood. Usually No. 3 tacks will be adequate for the muslin and No. 4 tacks will be adequate for the upholstering fabric. You should be careful to place the tacks holding the upholstering fabric in a straight line along the edge within about ¼ inch of the line where the excess of fabric will be trimmed off after tacking is completed because you will expect to cover all tack heads as well as the clipped edge of the fabric with gimp which is about ½ inch wide.

You should purchase gimp which will match your fabric as closely as possible. The gimp is applied with white glue after you have trimmed the excess fabric below the tacks. Add some white glue to about one inch of the inside of the gimp at an end which has been trimmed off square. Put it into place at the front edge of a back leg. Hold it in place with two pins, one inserted from above and the other from below to hold the gimp flat. Now apply glue from the bottle along about six inches of the gimp and carefully press in place, adding more pins as necessary to hold the gimp in place. Proceed in this manner until you reach the front edge of the other back leg and then cover the back portion between the legs. Do not use too much glue and be careful not to get glue on your fabric or on the outside surface of the gimp.

Figure 5.5 is a photograph of a chair with an upholstered seat. Although this upholstered seat appears to be quite deep there is only about one inch of padding under the cotton. The style of this chair is such that the upholstering is attached nearly at the bottom of the rails which are about 1½ inch wide.

The job should be finished by tacking a piece of black cambric to the bottom of the seat rails.

Fig. 5.5 Photograph of a small chair with upholstered seat.

Chairs with Upholstered Seat and Back

Chairs which have an upholstered seat with an upholstered back panel are quite common. The upholstering of the seat is carried out by the the same procedure as that used with small chairs except that the padding of the seat is usually thicker. Many of these chairs have arms and the fabric must be folded around the front arm supports by the same method as that used to fold it around the back legs. If plastic foam is used for the padding, the two inch thickness will usually be appropriate.

The back panel will have upholstering on both sides and it is necessary to use webbing to support the padding. It is not possible to stretch the webbing across the opening because it must be tacked to the inside of the opening. Figure 5.6 shows a cross section of the opening showing how the webbing is attached. The upholstering fabric is to be tacked to the surfaces A. The webbing, B, must be stretched as tightly as possible by hand and tacked with the tacks, C, and burlap D is then tacked in place on the front side of the webbing. The padding is placed on the front side of the burlap and is indicated at E. The padding is usually about one inch or more thick and consists of the same kind of padding as that used in the seat with a layer of cotton over it. The padding is then covered with un-bleached muslin, F, and upholstering fabric, G_1, which are tacked to the surfaces, A. Upholstering fabric G_2 is also tacked to the surfaces, A, on the back. Gimp is then attached to the edges in the same manner as it is attached around the seat. When you glue the gimp to the edges of the front, put newspaper over the seat to protect it from glue which might drip on it.

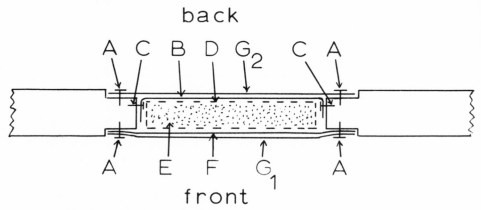

Fig. 5.6 Cross section sketch of an upholstered chair back.

Fig. 5.7 Upholstered rocker with removable cushion and back.

Another type of chair which falls in this general category has a removable cushion. In this case there is a separate wood frame on which the padding is placed and the upholstering fabric is stretched over the padding and tacked to the underside of the frame. Figure 5.7 is a photograph of a rocker of this type. This rocker also has a removable frame in the back which is attached to the side pieces with screws after the upholstering on the front of the frame is completed. After the frame is secured in place with the screws, the back upholstering is tacked in place to the side pieces of the chair. In some instances, gimp would be used to cover the tacks which secure the back upholstering but with this chair, which is quite delicate, I folded the edges of the back upholstering fabric under and tacked it in place with gimp tacks. Gimp tacks have small round heads which are not very obvious against the upholstering fabric. Their name derives from the fact that they were used for attaching gimp before suitable glue was available.

Upholstered Furniture with Built-up Spring Seats Without Separate Cushions

Most large upholstered chairs and couches have coil springs, supported on webbing, which, in turn, support the padding. There are usually three side-to-side rows of springs in the seat and the number of front-to-back rows will depend on the length of the seat. The distance between centers of the springs should be determined when the seat is dismantled, but if this was not possible, you can determine the proper spacings by laying out the springs on an area having the same dimensions as the frame of the chair seat.

The webbing is stretched and tacked to the bottom of the frame with the centers of the webbing strips in each direction on the same lines as the centers of the springs so that each spring will rest on the area where the webbing strips cross. The method of stretching and tacking the webbing is described in an earlier section, and Figure 5.4 shows the process of stretching and tacking the webbing. Figure 5.8 shows a view from the top showing how the springs are attached to the webbing by sewing with linen cord.

After all of the springs have been attached to the webbing, they must be tied in order to force them to act in unison so that a load applied at one point will be distributed over the surrounding springs. The springs should be tied so that the top surface will be as flat as possible.

The tying is started by attaching a heavy jute or reinforced cotton cord to the top of the rail, opposite a front-to-back row of springs, as shown in Figure 5.8, leaving a free end about ten inches long. The cord is tied around the second coil of the spring while it is held compressed about 1½ inches from the top. It is then tied to the top coil of the spring on the opposite side, then to the near side top coil of the second spring and so on, finishing with the second coil on the far side of the last spring. The cord is

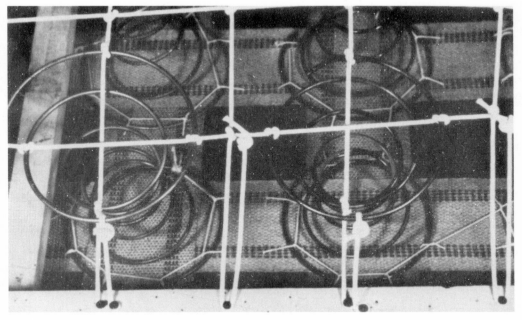

Fig. 5.8 Photograph of a portion of a spring assembly showing a method of attaching the springs to the webbing
and the method of tying the springs.

then tacked to the opposite rail with the tension such that
the row of springs will be symmetrical and the cord is cut
off leaving a free end about ten inches long. The free ends
are then tied to the top coils of the springs on the ends of
the row. The successive front-to-back rows are tied in the
same manner being careful to keep the tensions in the
cords such that the levels of the springs in all of the rows
are the same. When the front-to-back rows are all tied, the
side-to-side rows are tied together in the same manner.
Figure 5.8 shows a portion of a spring seat with the springs
tied. The whole assembly will be more completely inter-
locked by adding a cord tied to the cords, which are tied
to the springs, between each two rows of springs as indicated in Figure 5.8. All cords should be attached to the
frame with No. 14 tacks and two such tacks should be used
at the ends of the cords tied to the springs.

When the springs are all properly tied, the top surface
of the spring assembly is covered with burlap which should
be stretched tight and tacked to the top edge of the frame
with No. 4 tacks. Even though you tied the springs so that
the top surface of the spring assembly is as flat as possible,
it will still be rounded and slope toward the edges as indicated in Figure 5.9.

Fig. 5.9 Sketch showing the contour of a spring seat after the
springs are tied and the burlap is tacked in place.

It is necessary to correct this condition before adding
the padding or the seat will not be comfortable to sit on.
The method of correction is illustrated in Figure 5.10.
Figure 5.10A shows an additional strip of burlap about
10 to 12 inches wide tacked to the frame of the seat with
a layer of upholstering moss placed between the burlap
cover for the springs and this supplementary burlap strip.
The moss should be distributed as evenly as possible along
the edge and the burlap strip is folded over it and sewed
to the burlap spring cover along the line A in Figure 5.10A
using a large curved upholstering needle and heavy linen

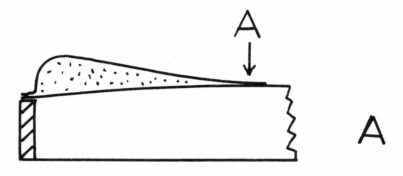

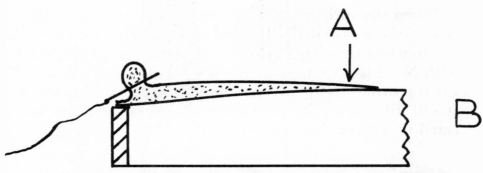

Fig. 5.10 Sketch showing the method of building up the edges of a spring seat.

cord. A roll along the edge is formed by bunching the moss tightly under the burlap strip and sewing with a large straight upholstering needle with the linen cord as indicated in Figure 5.10B. The top of the roll should be about even with the level of the top of the springs in the center of the frame. Figure 5.11 is a photograph of a chaise lounge with this step completed.

The next step in forming the seat is to add the padding. As in the case of the small chairs, this padding may be moss, plastic foam, or rubberized curly hair. The padding should be two to three inches thick, depending on the piece, and the eastiest material to use is the plastic foam which can be easily cut to the exact shape of the seat. If moss is used it must be uniformly distributed.

After the padding is properly arranged, it should be covered with a layer of upholstering cotton and an un-bleached muslin cover should be cut using the original fabric as a pattern and the muslin is stretched over the padding and tacked in place in a manner similar to that described in an earlier section. Figure 5.12 shows the chaise lounge with the muslin tacked in place.

The arms and back usually have webbing and burlap attached in a manner similar to that illustrated in Figure 5.6. Each piece of furniture presents a different problem and the method used by the original craftsman should be

Fig. 5.11 Photograph of a Chaise Lounge after the edges of the seat have been built up.

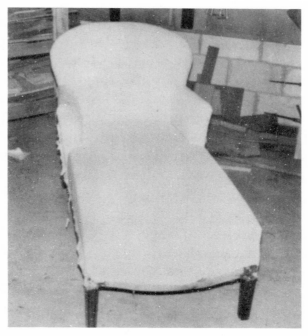

Fig. 5.12 Photograph of a Chaise Lounge after the padding and muslin have been applied.

followed. Often the padding for these areas can be reused, but some supplementary material is usually needed, especially on top of the arms. Although any of the types of padding can be used, I prefer to use moss as it is easier to build it up to form the desired shape. After the padding on the back and arms is properly formed, they are covered with cotton and muslin. The most convenient order is usually to do the arms, securing the padding with cotton and muslin, and then to do the back. The chaise lounge shown in Figure 5.12 has the padding on the arms and back completed with the muslin cover in place. Three inch plastic foam was used on the seat, and moss, recovered when the piece was dismantled, was used on the back and arms. The seat must be built high enough so that there will be no visible gap between the seat and the back and arms.

The fabric should be cut using the original fabric pieces as patterns but the new pieces should be cut somewhat larger than the patterns to allow some leeway for adjusting the pieces in place. It is desirable to lay out the entire piece of upholstering fabric and pin the patterns to it in preparation for cutting. Normally the lengthwise direction of the fabric extends from front to back on the seat and from bottom to top of the back and from inside bottom up over the top and down outside the arms. If the fabric has a pattern such as flowers, the bottom of the pattern should be at the front of the seat and at the bottom of the back and arms. A bouquet of flowers does not look right upside down.

The seat and back of a large couch will often be wider than the width of the fabric. The full width of the fabric should be centered on the seat and back and separate pieces can then be sewed to each side to extend the width enough so that the ends can be tacked in place. If the fabric has lengthwise stripes, the line of the seam should be selected so that the sequence of the pattern will be continuous over the seam. This can be assured if the pieces are pinned together before sewing on a sewing machine. The seam must be straight and parallel to the lines of the pattern. Remember also that the arms are mirror images of each other so that a fabric with a pattern of stripes of different colors should run in one direction around one arm and in the opposite direction around the other arm so that the sequence of colors from front to back will be the same on both arms. For example, a couch or chair with a fabric having red, white and blue stripes will not look right if the sequence from back to front is red, white and blue on one arm and blue, white and red on the other. You should study your fabric carefully before you do any cutting to be certain that you cut the various pieces so that the arrangement of pattern on the finished piece will be logical.

Figure 5.13 shows a couch with the upholstering completed. The upholstering of the seat on this couch is quite straightforward but there is a special technique, which is often encountered, involved with the arms. The arms have wood panels on the front so the fabric which is applied to the arms must end at the back of this panel. However, this would make it necessary to cover the tack heads and the raw edge of the fabric with gimp. This is usually not done on areas which are subject to wear, as the wearing quality of gimp is generally not as good as that of the fabric. The procedure for attaching the fabric is, therefore, that illustrated in Figure 5.14. In this illustration, the panel on the front of the arm is indicated at A, B is the fabric, and C is a strip of cardboard about ¾ inch wide. Tacks, D, are driven through the cardboard and the fabric at about 1½ inch intervals with the cardboard held so that its edge holds the fabric tight against the inside edge of the front panel. In some instances, depending on the shape of the arm, the single piece of fabric with the cardboard strip will extend all the way up on the inside of the

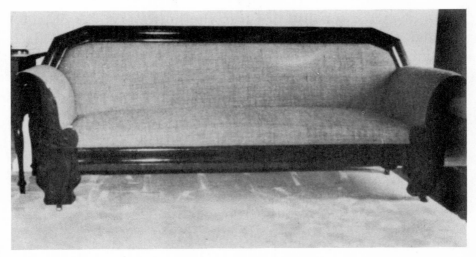

Fig. 5.13 Photograph of a large upholstered couch with a built up spring seat.

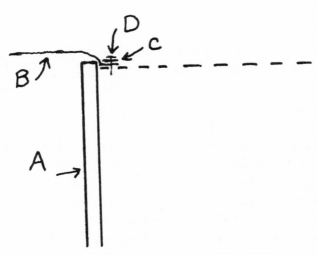

Fig. 5.14 Sketch showing a method of attaching the fabric at the front of the arm of the couch shown in Fig. 5.13.

arm, over the top and down to the bottom on the outside. Usually, however, the arm is shaped so that the one piece of fabric covers the inside, over the top and around the curve of the arm to the point where the curvature reverses, as shown in Figure 5.15, which is a front view of the arm. The one strip of fabric will extend from A to B and another piece of fabric will extend from B to C. The top of this piece of fabric may be attached using a cardboard strip where the top edge is turned under.

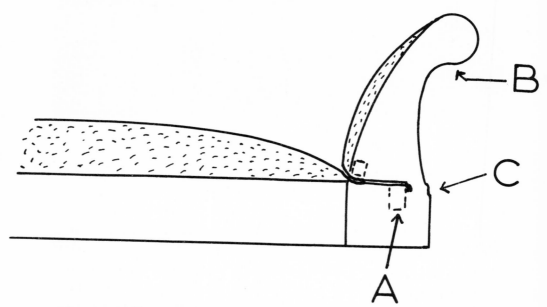

Fig. 5.15 Sketch showing how the fabric is applied around the arm of the couch in Fig. 5.13.

When the fabric with its cardboard strip is tacked in place around the arm, a strip of cotton is laid over the cardboard and the fabric is folded back over the arm and stretched in place so that, at all points, it fits snugly over the padding and is secured with tacks at A and B. The couch shown in Figure 5.13 has a removable frame on which the back upholstering is mounted.

Figure 5.16 is an old-fashioned love seat in which the

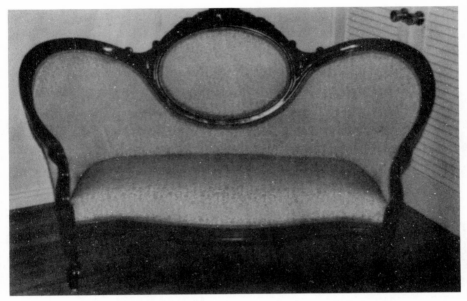

Fig. 5.16 Photograph of an upholstered love seat.

upholstering of the seat is done in the same manner as that of the large couch. The back of this kind of piece, however, presents a special problem. The back, next to the ends, is concave on the front side in the horizontal plane. When the fabric is extended down back of the seat, it passes under a large steel wire, A, in Figure 5.17, which is a cross section of the love seat, and is attached to the frame at B. The back of the love seat, however, is convex so a distance the fabric must cover along B is greater than a corresponding distance along A so it will be necessary to slit the fabric at approximately one inch intervals up to, *but not beyond,* the point where it passes under the wire at A. It is important to remember that these slits will show when someone sits on the love seat if the seat is not built up high enough. This factor must be kept in mind when the padding on the seat is being built up. This type of furniture is very difficult to upholster so that the fabric on the back will lie flat on the padding without wrinkling. The pieces of fab-

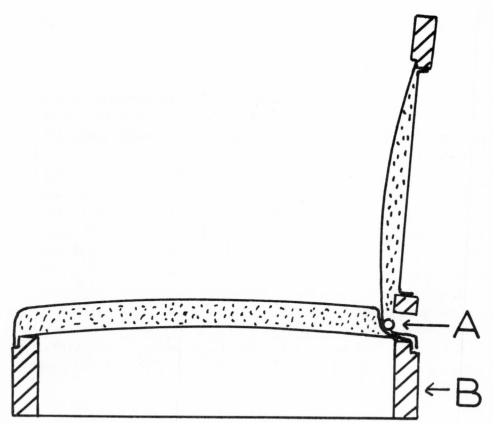

Fig. 5.17 Sketch showing how the fabric is attached on the back of the love seat shown in Fig. 5.16.

ric should be cut oversize to give you a chance to move them around in order to obtain a good wrinkle-free fit. Most such furniture is too wide for a single width of fabric to cover the entire back. It is best to plan the cutting so that the seams are near the narrow portion of the fabric.

Upholstered Furniture with Built-up Spring Seats with Separate Cushions

Chairs and couches with separate cushions require the same procedure for attaching the webbing, installing and tying the springs and installing the burlap as those not having separate cushions. It is particularly important to build up the front edge of the seat to a level at least equal to that of the center of the spring assembly (*see* Fig. 5.10) or the cushion will tend to slide off the front of the seat.

When the preparation of the seat has progressed to the stage indicated in Figure 5.11, about one inch of cotton should be laid over the burlap and covered with unbleached muslin.

A wing chair is a good example of this type of upholstered furniture and it furnishes examples of several upholstering problems not considered before. It is particularly important, when working with a complicated piece such as this, to study the way in which the original upholstering was done. It may even be desirable to leave the upholstering on one wing and arm until you have prepared the padding and tacked the muslin in place on the other side.

Figure 5.18 is a cross section view through the wing, arm and seat of such a chair which shows the method of construction. The webbing and burlap B (Fig. 5.18) are attached to the inside of the frame in the same manner as that indicated in Figure 5.6. In some instances the webbing is omitted and only burlap is used. The muslin, D. (Fig. 5.18) is attached to the outside of the top of the frame at A, brought over the top of the frame, which should have a thin layer of cotton padding over it, brought down over the padding and attached at E. It is then passed around and attached at the back of the frame of the wing in the same manner as it is attached at E. Some careful cutting and folding will be required at the top back and bottom back corners similar to the fitting and folding at the legs of the small chair seat. The front of the wing is rounded so that the fabric can be folded around it with a very minor amount of tucking. Both wings should be completed to the stage where they are covered with muslin and you should be careful to have the same amount of padding on both so that they will be symmetrical.

When the wings have been covered on the inside with padding and muslin, the padding and muslin should be attached to the inside and top of the arms. The muslin,

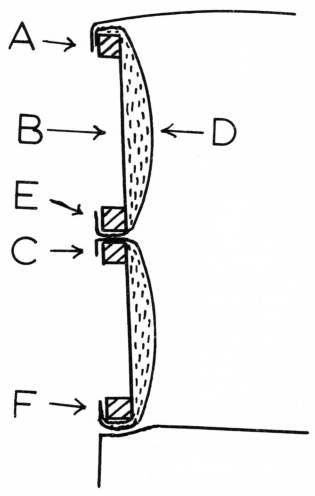

Fig. 5.18 Sketch showing the method of applying the padding
on the wing and arm of a wing chair.

and later the fabric, is attached at C in Figure 5.18 and the
padding on the top of the arm should be thick enough so
that there will be a tight fit between the top of the arm
and the bottom of the wing. It will be necessary to cut
a slit in the muslin to accommodate the front frame of the
wing where it is attached to the top of the arm frame. The
lower end of the muslin is passed between the lower frame
and the seat and is attached at F. In the back, it will pass

between the arm padding and the back padding and will be tacked to the back of the arm frame. In the front, the muslin is folded around and tacked to the front of the arm frame. It will be necessary to fold in a series of small tucks as the muslin is folded around the front of the arm frame. When both arms have been padded and covered with muslin the inside of the back should be built up. Many of these chairs have springs in the back which are attached to webbing and tied in the same manner as the seat springs. Although we correct for the curvature of the spring system in the seat, we do not do so in the back because the back should have some bulge in the center. After the padding has been built up in the back, it is covered with cotton and muslin which is tacked to the outside of the top back frame and on the sides it is passed between the back padding and the wing and arm padding and tacked to the back of the frame on the side. Care must be exercised in cutting and folding at the top corners. The back padding must be thick enough at the sides so that there will be a tight fit between the muslin on the back and that on the wings and arms. At the bottom, the muslin is pulled around the bottom of the back frame and tacked in the same manner as the muslin covering the arms was tacked at F. You should use the same care in fitting the muslin as you will later use in fitting the fabric in order to have a smooth surface over which the fabric will be fitted and also to provide you with experience in fitting before you begin to work with the more expensive fabric. No muslin is used on the outside of the wings, arms and back but burlap with a layer of cotton sewed to the oustide is often used.

You are now ready to cut and fit the fabric. The same precautions regarding proper orientation of your patterns on the fabric which were given in the previous section also apply here. You should first fit the fabric on the inside of the wings and then on the inside and over the top

of the arms. At the point where the top of an arm inter-
sects the front of the wing the fabric must be folded in
between the padding on the arm and the front frame of
the wing as illustrated in Figure 5.19. The inside of the
back is then covered with the fabric fitted just as the
muslin was fitted. You may find that some small tucks
are necessary as you fit the fabric over the top of the back
frame. The seat may be covered with the upholstering
fabric but if you are using an expensive fabric you can
make a saving by using an inexpensive strong fabric with
a strip of your upholstering fabric sewed to the front of

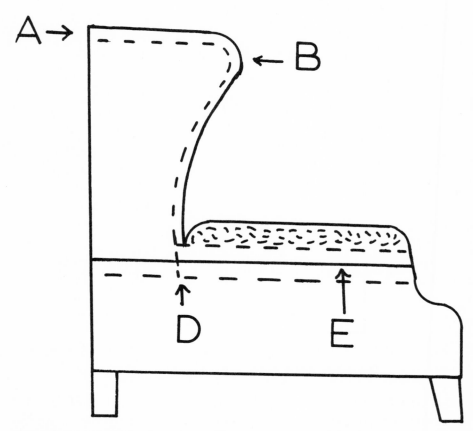

Fig. 5.19 Sketch showing the arrangement of the sections of
fabric on the side of a wing chair.

it where it shows under the front of the cushion. Most chairs of this type have a front arrangement similar to that shown in Figure 5.20 where the seat is indicated at A, and the arms are indicated at B and B'. The line, C, is at the level of the base of the arms and the front edge of the seat fabric is tacked below this line.

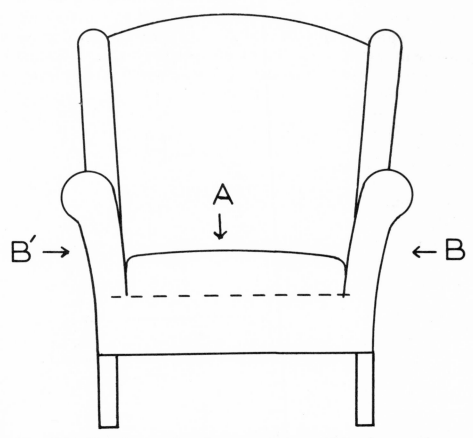

Fig. 5.20 Sketch showing the arrangement of the bottom front of an upholstered chair.

You have now reached the stage where it will be necessary to prepare fabric covered cording to be attached before the rest of the upholstering fabric can be installed. To prepare the cording, cut a strip of the upholstering fabric on the bias about 1¾ inches wide and sew it around the cord. The cording can be purchased at any drygoods store or you may be able to recover it from the old upholstering when you take it apart. The method of sewing the fabric around the cord is illustrated in Figure 5.21. A sewing machine with a zipper foot must be used so that the fabric can be sewed as close to the cord as possible. In Figure 5.21, A is the cord, B is the fabric, C is the sewing machine needle and D is the zipper foot. It will be necessary to prepare several yards of fabric covered cording for some pieces of furniture so it is necessary to sew strips of the bias cut fabric together to form a great enough length to do the job. You can cut strips from scraps and sew them together to form the necessary lengths or you can prepare a strip by a method which I will describe in the next section.

You are now ready to cover the bottom front of the chair. Attach a piece of fabric covered cording with its top along the line, C, in Figure 5.20 with tacks spaced at about two inch intervals. Cut a straight piece of cardboard about ¾ inch wide and as long as the width of the chair along the line C in Figure 5.20. Place the edge of the fabric which is to cover the front bottom of the chair under the cardboard and push the fabric up against the cording as indicated in Figure 5.22 and tack the cardboard

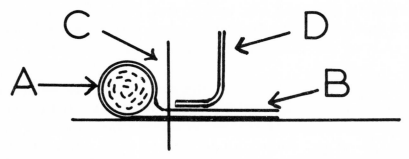

Fig. 5.21 Method of sewing a bias strip of fabric around the cording.

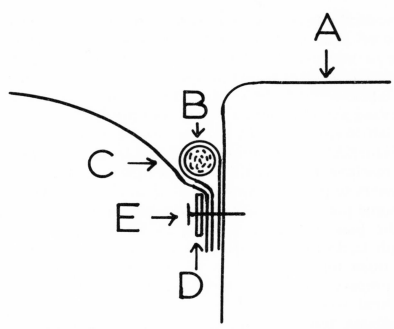

Fig. 5.22 Sketch showing the method of attaching fabric at the bottom front of an upholstered chair.

and fabric in place. In Figure 5.22, A is the top of the chair seat, B is the cording, C is the piece of fabric which will cover the lower portion of the chair front, D is the cardboard strip and E represents the tacks which will hold the cardboard and the fabric in place. The fabric must be oriented so that when it is folded down over the cardboard strip the right side will be out. Now fold the fabric down and tack under the front edge of the seat and bend the ends of the fabric around the sides of the chair and tack.

The next step is to cover the outside of the wings. If padding is to be used, cut a piece of burlap to fit the area, lightly sew a layer of cotton to the burlap and tack the burlap in place. Referring to Figure 5.19, an end of a piece of fabric covered cording is attached around the back at A and is attached with tacks along the top edge of the wing, around at B and down the edge of the wing to D. Space the tacks at about two inch intervals and about ¼ inch from the line of the seam shown in Figure 5.21. The cording should be tacked in place so that the top of the cord is even with the edge of the wing. Now trace out the shape of the wing just inside the cord and cut a strip of cardboard about ¾ inch wide which will fit right up to the cording around the wing. The fabric for the outside of the wing is now tacked in place by folding the edge under the cardboard and tacking through the cardboard and fabric, starting at B. (*See* Fig. 5.22 for details of the use of cardboard to hold the fabric against the cording.) Add tacks at about 1½ inch intervals on each side of B progressing toward A and D. Test after the first two or three tacks have been driven in to be certain that the fabric has been properly oriented and that it will cover the wing without wrinkling. Finish by bending the fabric around the back frame and tacking and also by tacking along the horizontal line passing through D.

To cover the lower portion of the sides, cut a strip of cardboard the length of the line E in Fig. 5.19 and attach the lower side panels of the fabric using the cardboard strip in the same way that it was used to attach the top of the fabric on the lower front of the chair. The top edge of the cardboard should be along the line E. After the cardboard and fabric have been tacked in place, fold the fabric down over the cardboard and tack under the bottom edge of the chair and around the back of the arm. Do not attach the fabric at the front of the arm as this will be taken care of later. If the outside of the arm is to be padded follow the same procedure as that for the outside of the wings.

A length of fabric covered cording is tacked in place on the back, starting at the bottom on one side, extending up to the top corner, across the top and down to the bottom on the other side. The cording should be placed so that the round portion is right at the edge. The cording should be tacked at no more than 1½ inch intervals along the two sides but two inch intervals are adequate across the top. Now cut a strip of cardboard shaped so that it will fit against the round portion of the cording across the top of the back and attach the top edge of the back piece of fabric by tacking through the cardboard and fabric. (*See* Fig. 5.22) Start with a tack at the center and one at each end and then fold the fabric over to test whether it is straight with respect to the back of the chair. Remember that if the fabric has lengthwise stripes it will be necessary to orient the top of this piece very accurately or the stripes will not run vertically on the back. If it is straight fold it back and add tacks about every 1½ inch. The side edges of the back panel are then folded under and sewed to the cording on the two sides using a small curved upholstering needle and thread which matches the fabric. To get a nice tight fit of the back panel, fold the edge under and pin it in place at several points on each side. When the back panel is completely sewed in place on both sides, the bottom edge should be tacked to the bottom of the chair frame.

The front surfaces of the arms are covered by first tacking fabric covered cording around the contour of the front surface and attaching a piece of fabric which has been cut so that it will fit the area enclosed by the cording with the edges folded under. This piece of fabric is then sewed to the cording. In some instances some cotton padding is placed under this piece of fabric while in others a piece of cardboard is cut to fit the area enclosed by the cording and the fabric is folded around the cardboard and then sewed to the cording with the small curved needle. If the front of the arms is very narrow, the fabric is folded around it and no cording is used as indicated in Fig. 5.25. The front edges of the bottom side pieces are now folded under so that the edge of the fold is at the cording and they are sewed to the cording with the small curved needle.

Some old chairs have cushions stuffed with feathers and

some have a built up spring system covered with the upholstering fabric. Neither of these methods of forming a cushion is as good as a plastic foam filled cushion. In many cases it is possible to purchase a plastic foam filler already cut to the proper size. If your chair is not a standard size, you can cut a piece of three inch plastic foam to fit the chair and then cover it with the fabric.

The strip which goes around the edges of the cushion should be cut one inch wider than the thickness of the cushion in order to allow for ½ inch seams on both sides. The top and bottom pieces are also cut one inch larger each way for the same reason. Enough fabric covered cording is prepared to go all the way around the cushion at both the top and bottom edges. With the cover inside out, the seams are pinned together with the cording between the edge fabric and the top and bottom pieces. This is then sewed all the way around on a sewing machine with a zipper foot, sewing through the four thicknesses of fabric, except that along one edge on one side the cording is sewed only to the side fabric so that the cover can be turned back right side out and the foam filler can be inserted. After the filler is inserted the edge fabric is sewed to the cording with the curved needle to finish closing the cover of the cushion.

Figure 5.23 is a photograph of a wing chair with the upholstering completed. Figure 5.24 is a photograph of another type of upholstered chair. Note that the chair in Fig. 5.24 does not have separate wings so the fabric covering the arms must be sewed to that covering the upper side pieces with cording incorporated in the seam. In order to locate the seam on such a chair the two pieces of fabric are temporarily tacked in place to be certain that they will fit and the edges at the seam are folded under so that the folded edges just come together where the seam will be located. Pins can be inserted along the edges to mark their exact position or they can be marked with chalk. One point

Fig. 5.23 Photograph of an upholstered wing chair.

Fig. 5.24 Photograph of an upholstered chair without separate wings.

near the middle where the two pieces will come together should be marked on both pieces and they are then removed from the chair and pinned together along the line of the seam with fabric covered cording between them. Sew the seam with a sewing machine using a zipper foot so the seam will be as close as possible to the cord.

Figure 5.25 is a more modern type of upholstered chair. Note that the fabric covering the arms on both sides is sewed to the back fabric with cording in the seam. This is done in a manner similar to the forming of the seam on the arm of the chair in Fig. 5.24 except that it is necessary to locate these seams with a higher accuracy than was necessary in doing the seams on the arms of the chair in Fig. 5.24. Note also that this chair has narrow arms and the inside arm fabric is folded over the front of the arm and tacked on the outside of the frame and a fold is made on the top front of the arm similar to that at the front of the small chair illustrated in Fig. 5.5.

Fig. 5.25 Photograph of a modern type of upholstered chair.

Preparation of Bias Strip to Cover Cording

The preparation of a bias strip of the fabric to cover cording was mentioned in the previous section. To prepare such a strip, you can cut pieces of the fabric on the bias and sew them together. However, this is difficult to do since it is difficult to sew the separate pieces together so that the strip will be straight.

The following method is quite easy and it yields long bias strips, all sewed together, with a relatively few simple operations. You should start with a rectangular piece of the fabric cut out so that the threads in the fabric are parallel to the sides. Place the piece of fabric on a table, right side up. (*See* Fig. 5.26) Fold the fabric along the line AA′ which is the center line on the long length of the rectangle. The edge BB′ will then fall along the edge CC′,

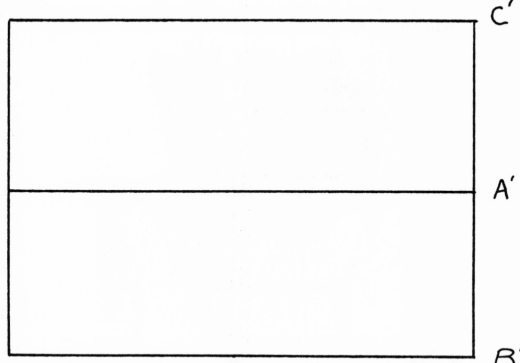

Fig. 5.26 Sketch showing a piece of fabric to be used for preparing a bias strip.

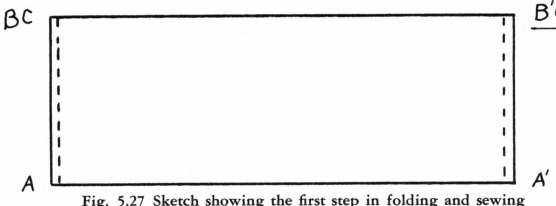

Fig. 5.27 Sketch showing the first step in folding and sewing a piece of fabric for making a bias strip.

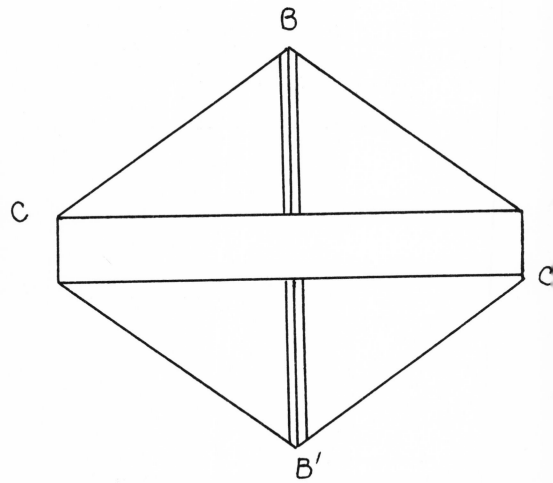

Fig. 5.28 Sketch showing the second step in folding a piece of fabric for making a bias strip.

as in Fig. 5.27. Sew a seam with the sewing machine along each end of the folded piece. The seam should be about ⅜ inch from the ends and the thread should match the fabric. These seams are indicated by the dotted lines in Fig. 5.27.

Now grasp the centers of the two sides and spread them open so that the piece takes the shape shown in Fig. 5.28. The seams will be on top with their ends at B and B′. The fabric at the ends should be snipped with scissors down to the seams so that they will lie flat and the seams should be pressed. Now cut along the folds CB and C′B′ so that the fabric can be folded out to the shape shown in Fig. 5.29. The fabric is now right side up, B and B′ are the original seams and the arrows on the lines in the center of the figure indicate the directions of the threads in the fabric.

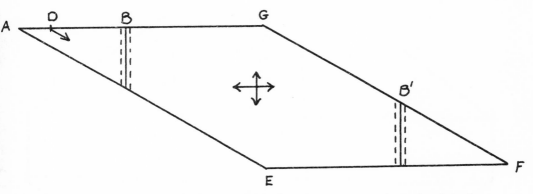

Fig. 5.29 Sketch showing the third step in preparing the fabric for making a bias strip.

You must now decide about the width of the bias strip which you are going to cut and locate the point D such that AD is equal to that width. Now fold the edge EF over on to the edge DG so that E falls on D and F projects beyond G by the same amount that A projects beyond D. Pin these edges together and sew a seam with the sewing machine about ⅜ inch from the edge. This will form an awkward appearing tube of the fabric. Now start at D and with your scissors cut along the line indicated with an arrow in Fig. 5.29, maintaining the same width of strip around and around the tube until you finally end at G. You now have a bias strip with all pieces sewed together properly and with no waste. As an example, I started with a piece of material 15 x 18 inches, and from this I was able to cut a bias strip 1¾ inches wide and four yards long.

Index